POLITICS IN THE TRENCHES

POLITICS IN THE TRENCHES

Citizens, Politicians, and the Fate of Democracy

THOMAS J. VOLGY

The University of Arizona Press

Tucson

The University of Arizona Press

© 2001 The Arizona Board of Regents

All rights reserved

♾ This book is printed on acid-free, archival-quality paper.

Manufactured in the United States of America

06   05   04   03   6   5   4   3

Library of Congress Cataloging-in-Publication Data

Volgy, Thomas J.

  Politics in the trenches : citizens, politicians, and the fate of
democracy / Thomas J. Volgy.

      p. cm.

Includes bibliographical references.

ISBN 0-8165-2085-2 (cloth : acid-free paper)

ISBN 0-8165-2086-0 (paper : acid-free paper)

  1. Democracy—United States.   2. Political culture—United States.
3. Politicians—United States.   4. Political planning—United States.
5. Political participation—United States.   I. Title.

JK1726.V65 2001

320.973—dc21   00-010454

British Library Cataloguing-in-Publication Data

A catalogue record for this book is available from the British Library.

To
Sharon Douglas,
who is teaching me once more how to love
and to see poetry in life,
and to
Matthew Metcalfe,
who is teaching me parenting and who will inherit
all the good and bad we leave for him
in the new millennium.

Contents

ACKNOWLEDGMENTS

When you try to balance three lives and you have been a citizen of two different countries, either you go crazy or you survive because of the kindness and understanding of your friends and loved ones. I would like to thank my friends and family, who have always understood, and have been there for me, even when I wasn't there for them. Special thanks go to Jerry Anderson; Garry Bryant and Margy McGonagill; Sylvia Carbajal; Arthur and Barbara Dubow; Sandy Volgy; June and Paul Eisland; Gary Grynkewich; Gabor Harangozo; Gulnara Kurmanova; Dana Larsen; Jan Lesher; Larry Morris and Patti Mathes; John Schwarz, who was once a mentor and is now a colleague and a great friend; Judy Schwarz; David Spiro; Nick Vitale; and LaMonte Ward and the rest of the poker group: Jefferson Carter, John Crow, J. T. Fey, Stuart Goldberg, Kirby Lockard, and Jan Wezelman. I owe more than thanks to my family: Edit Volgyi and Imre Volgyi (posthumously) and Peter Rejto.

INTRODUCTION

On a wet and cold November night in 1956, while dodging a hail of bullets fired at them by Russian soldiers, my parents successfully crossed the border into Austria from Hungary and escaped the deadly Soviet fires that burned to cinders the Hungarian revolution. Once out of Hungary, they decided that there was only one place they could go to start a new life: America. America was the land of opportunity. America was the one and only place in the world where they could hope to have their immigrant child take his place among those who were born to their citizenship, and equally to enjoy the fruits of being an American.

And so we came to America. It turns out that my parents were correct about my chances. I became the first in the family to go to college (no one else had gone beyond the ninth grade), and success in college led to a Ph.D. The immigrant child became a professor, an activist, a writer, and mayor of the thirtieth largest city in the United States.

For me, the American dream of opportunity resulting from hard work has been fulfilled. My parents were less fortunate, and their travails taught me much about how hard it can be to survive in America. Our experiences taught me as well about the crucial importance of politics and government in creating real opportunity for all Americans. Without the appropriate public policies, my own opportunities would have come to naught. And because some public policies didn't exist, my parents' lives were at times unbearable. My father could not pay for the type of health care commonly available to those who can afford being part of the best health care system in the world, and it eventually killed him. When national economic policies failed to provide decent jobs at decent wages, my parents floundered on the seas of the working poor, unable to translate hard work and persistence into anything more than an abysmal existence.

My own little family became a laboratory of what was possible in America. And through it I found myself becoming involved with politics and government, and while struggling with myriad societal problems, I learned to treasure the importance of democracy to our American way of life. I spent fourteen years in elected office, and through persistent contacts with the people who run local and national governments I learned a deep appreciation not only of the way in which we pursue public policies but also of the honesty, courage, integrity, and dedication of the men and women who give content, and flesh and blood, to the words *politics* and *government*.

Both as a citizen and as an elected official, I came to learn as well about the importance of "political culture" in our lives. Democracy is hard work for both politicians and citizens. Attitudes toward politics, politicians, and government are deeply engrained in the American culture. Citizens don't go into the voting booth naked; they enter with deep-seated expectations about the political system. Neither do they watch the news or read newspapers with a blank slate. They "see" with the lenses of prior expectations, desires, and disgusts about the political system. In turn, the political culture is not static; it changes with myriad collective experiences from everyday life. Unfortunately, too little of the ebb and flow of what government officials do actually get to be viewed by citizens. Their collective experiences have come increasingly from media translations of the most cartoonish kind.

The purpose of this book is not to write another "kiss and tell" story about one politician's experiences. Instead, the objective is to convey the trials and tribulations of elected officials as they go about the task of fulfilling their responsibilities. Apart from the personal gratification for doing so, my primary intent is to offer to readers a window on the political world that is seldom available to most citizens. Such a window should create a better understanding of who our representatives are, what hurdles they face in trying to do a "good" job, and what happens when we fail to understand how we treat our politicians and how such treatment affects the quality of politics, government, and public policy.

There are many flaws in our political process, and many mistakes are being made in our public policies. All of them are correctable as long as citizens believe in the essential worth of the political system itself. I fear, though, that such beliefs are substantially eroding. With such erosion comes a threat to our democracy and the American way of life. This book was developed to offer a perspective on democratic governance that is rarely seen in public view: While it recognizes many of the flaws in politics, it seeks to show as well that those who govern are not liars, crooks, and cheats. It is based on the premise that today's version of American democracy requires citizens to have a sense of *empathy* toward politicians. That empathy is nearly lost now, and the only way it can be reestablished is through citizens seeing what political actors do and by coming to understand who the elected officials are and how hard their representatives work with the tools they have.

It is rare to find a book that focuses on what the public does to its politicians. We have become so cynical about government that we instead typically look for how government and politicians have hurt us. Seldom, if ever, do we take the time to pay attention to the working conditions of those who represent us. Even those who know better— politicians and the media—have often failed to take the risks in speaking out against the onslaught. To the contrary, too many people in both media and politics have only encouraged this trend and have capitalized on it for personal or political gain. The popular books on our reading lists underline and exploit this growing unhappiness with politics. Have you read *Why Americans Hate Politics; Dirty Politics: Deception, Distraction and Democracy; The United States of Ambition; Malice in Wonderland: The Congressional Crook Book; America: What Went Wrong;* or *Who Will Tell the People: The Betrayal of American Democracy*?

No wonder, then, that many good people are retiring from public office. Recently, over 150 members of Congress chose voluntarily to vacate their elected offices. Scores of successful mayors and council members have decided that it is no longer worthwhile to hold elected office in city hall. Competition for state legislative seats is dwindling throughout the fifty states. "Combat fatigue" and "burnout" are now common words in the political lexicon. Unless this trend can be reversed, the quality of government and the people who serve in it may be permanently impaired.

I will show another view. It is a view based on evidence and observation, and stitched around the idea of re-creating empathy toward those working to represent us. I've tried to blend my life into its chapters to give some added flavor and color. But the story is far from being mine: The book is based on three sets of sources. First, it is based on a close reading and reinterpretation of the relevant literature on democratic processes and national and local politics. Second, it is based on participant observation (on my part) over a course of fourteen years. Third, and most important, it is based on interviews with over 300 elected officials, including mayors, council members, and members of Congress. The interviews were conducted as conversations over a period of seven years. They occurred over lunches, dinners, and drinks and as addenda to appointments made in the course of official business. Few of the people being interviewed knew at the time that their answers to questions and prompts would be part of this book. Therefore, unless their comments were already part of the public record, I have protected the anonymity of those surveyed by disguising their names and their places of residence.

The book is organized into nine chapters. Chapter 1 is autobiographical and explores what happened to many immigrants who came to adopt America as their country. It is also about how I found the American dream and what it cost my parents and is meant to give the reader insight into one person's motivation to become involved in politics and governance. Chapter 2 explores the nature of the democratic process, American style. It highlights the importance of empathy and understanding as crucial ingredients to the experimental process of democratic governance. Chapter 3 discusses the nature and characteristics of the men and women who work in our political system. Chapter 4 contrasts the perception with the reality of patterns of compensation, reward, and "perks" provided to elected officials, and the psychological value of elections. It focuses as well on the importance of campaign finance reform for preserving the political system. Chapter 5 peeks into a week in the life of a mayor. Chapter 6 looks at the process of experimentation in the political laboratory of democratic policy making. Chapter 7 highlights the difficulties of making policy in the democratic laboratory by focusing on one case: the development of policies to address the issue of homelessness. Chapter 8 examines the ways in which the media cover what happens in the political laboratory. Chapter 9 concludes with recommendations and observations about the future of democratic governance. Chapters 3 through 8 have a common theme of contrasting the perception of governance with the realities of governing. The last chapter is followed by an extensive bibliography that I normally would have cited throughout the chapters but that I chose to list at the end of the book to minimize clutter for the reader.

Unlike the other chapters, Chapter 1 is strictly autobiographical. Fearing a touch of vanity, I tried to avoid writing this chapter, but was persuaded by friends that it was important to do so. On reflection, I believe that writing it in this manner conveys to the reader a number of objectives I had in mind. First, I wanted to show that there still exists a path to the American dream even, perhaps especially, for immigrants. Second, I wanted to show how important that dream is and how it can be available for some and not for others, even in the same family. Third, I wanted to convey in as interesting a manner as possible the complex ways through which people become aware of the importance of politics for their lives and choose to do something about it.

I expect this book to have three audiences. Elected officials and political activists will read it to find references about their friends and enemies. Students of political science will look for insights about the democratic process and local governance. My hope, however, is that the primary readers will be people who—as citizens—continue to recognize their responsibilities in the great American experiment. Some of them will be people who want to fulfill their responsibilities to society but who are fed up with "politics." Others will be those who are actively involved and can't get enough of politics. The majority may be those people who have become politically passive but who continue to worry about what is wrong with our political system. If reading the pages that follow can create a little bit more empathy within that last group for those in politics, who act on our behalf, then writing this book will have been more than worth the effort.

POLITICS IN THE TRENCHES

I

Coming to America

Freedom didn't last very long: thirty days of joy and hope that would come to be known later as the Hungarian Revolution. It was a modern David and Goliath tale gone sour, acted out between the late fall of October and the coming of winter in November of 1956. Hungarians fought for their dreams, won, and then lost once more as Soviet tanks thundered back into the streets of Budapest, sweeping before them a ragged army of mostly civilian defenders.

I was in the fourth grade, and I watched this landmark event of my life unfold as a child assesses the footprints that history makes around him. I was overjoyed at the fact that I didn't have to take piano lessons anymore. I peeked around curtains at the drama of people shooting and killing each other in front of our apartment house. I pouted when my parents refused to allow me to go out and play soccer with my friends (who pouted as well in their homes).

My parents faced more important choices. My dad played a small role in the revolution but a role large enough for imprisonment once the Communists retook the reins of the state. And through some strange twist of fate, the day before the revolution started, my mom lost her temper and publicly humiliated a Communist official and was threatened with arrest. Now, the ancien régime was coming back and they were in trouble.

For my mom, the answer to our troubles was an obvious one. In another era she had lived and worked in Western Europe, loved all that was not Hungary, and always wanted to leave. My dad was less sure and fought against the inevitable. His life was one of enormous success followed by great tragedy followed by enormous success. Despite these failures and successes, he was respected and loved by his peers, and he loved the wonders of Budapest: its nightlife, its splendor, the warmth of its friendship networks. Leaving it meant leaving his life for something infinitely smaller and less desirable.

But there was little choice left now. The Russian ring was closing, and within days Hungary would be sealed off again from the free world. They decided to go. My father requisitioned a large truck of the type used to carry potatoes from villages to the city. He then forged identity papers for a driver to take the truck to the Austro-Hungarian border and found a driver who would make the run in exchange for some gold coins. With two other couples willing to risk their lives, we hid in the back of the truck and took off for Austria, literally carrying little more than the clothes on our backs.

We did bring with us a bit of insurance, though: several bottles of rum to use as a bribe in case we ran into Soviet patrols along the way. The bottles were placed on the seat next to the driver, and he had instructions to give them to anyone who tried to stop us. By the time we hit the Russian checkpoint, the driver had gotten well acquainted with the rum, and our lives were saved by his drunken aggressiveness. He showed the forged papers to the Russian lieutenant, and at the crucial moment when he should have offered the bribe, he mumbled a "nyet" when asked if there was anyone in the back of the truck. When the lieutenant peered in and saw seven pairs of eyes staring back at him, the driver popped the clutch and took off. The soldiers opened fire, and machine guns strafed us as we veered back and forth along the road. Amazingly, we were not hit, and fortunately for us, they had instructions to hold their positions and wait for "freedom fighters" coming the same way. We were on our way to the border.

Hours later, we arrived at a village on the Austro-Hungarian border. By this time our driver could barely see the road through his drunken haze. He dropped us off, wished us luck, and told us he would make a few more runs and then escape to the West. We learned from mutual friends years later that he was shot and killed on his next trip.

We were city people. We knew little about villages and borders. My parents had imagined that once we got to this village we would see signs that said "This way to freedom" or "If you go this way, it's still Hungary." There were no signs; there was only a village shrouded in darkness, its edges lit by Soviet patrols. The barking of border patrol guard dogs would break the periods of quiet, along with distant machine gun fire.

My dad found a farmer and asked for directions to the mayor's house. Once we found the mayor, we asked him for help. He told us that if we gave him all of the money we still had with us, he would find us guides to take us to the border. We agreed and an hour later he returned with three armed Hungarian soldiers. There are times in people's lives when reality turns surreal. This was one of them. Rather than shooting us, they said, "We are your guides." They took the last of our possessions and asked us to walk very quietly behind them. We marched in this manner until we reached the edge of the village. Then we crawled on our hands and knees toward an invisible line that was occasionally swept by searchlights and littered with the bodies of people who had been shot earlier. At some point, the lead soldier motioned us to stop. "We can't go farther," he said, "because beyond this point is no-man's-land and we will be shot by the Austrians if they see us in our uniforms. The Russians will shoot all of you and us as well if they spot us. Now you run as fast as you can. You run straight. Somewhere ahead of you is an Austrian village. May God go with you."

We ran and ran and ran, until my father could run no more. Then we walked on, while the men in the group half-carried, half-dragged my father. Finally, we saw the lights of a village. We were either lost or free. As we approached the village, we found ourselves facing uniforms and guns aimed at us by soldiers speaking German. We were free.

WHERE TO GO?

We discovered quickly that our story was not unique. There were 5,000 Hungarian refugees at the village where we had crossed the border. We were evacuated immediately for fear that the Russians would come across and massacre everyone. We were transported to Salzburg, where we learned that over a quarter of a million Hungarians had escaped to the West. Another half million were less lucky; some of them were killed, others captured and returned. Many went to jail; the more fortunate ones were consigned to miserable lives. In all, nearly one in ten Hungarians made a dash for freedom. We were the luckiest ones.

And now we had choices: Where were we going to begin life again?

My dad's preference was to stay in Europe. He saw himself as a European man who spoke seven languages (but not English), who was well accustomed to the culture of the European middle class, and who would be quite able to forge for himself and his family a new and comfortable existence. My mom wanted to come to America. For Hungarians, America was the promised land: a place where opportunity abounds, where people are judged by their dedication and commitment, where you can do anything! My father ridiculed the idea. He knew that at his age, without knowing English and having no money and no specialized skill, life would be very hard.

They decided to come to America anyway. Assessing their son's future made the difference. They believed—and rightly so—that there was no place else in the world where a young immigrant child could be accepted as a true citizen in his adopted country. In Sweden or France or Germany or England, they knew that not only they but I as well would be treated forever as foreigners. We could succeed financially in Europe but I would never be accepted into society. Maybe my children would be, but that was not acceptable to my parents.

So they took the plunge and decided to go to a country they knew would be most difficult for them to go to—for the sake of their child. Fortunately, the American government passed a special immigration law, allowing 10,000 Hungarian refugees to come to the United States if they met certain special requirements, including having family and institutional sponsors. We qualified, and by late December of 1956 we were on our way to America.

COMING TO AMERICA

We saw New York City for the first time on New Year's Eve. Hundreds of thousands of people clustered around Times Square in joyous, drunken celebration of the New Year. "Edit," my father said, "maybe this wasn't such a bad choice after all. These people know how to party like Europeans. Do you think it's like this every week?"

We learned quickly that there would be little partying and that life for immigrants is very difficult. With no money, no language, and no knowledge of how the country worked, my parents started nonetheless with enthusiasm and hope. Our distant relatives living in New York—and fearing that we would mooch off of them—bought us three one-

way train tickets to Corpus Christi, Texas, where a religious organization offered to sponsor us. Our relatives told us that in Texas the streets
were paved with gold and opportunity existed around every corner. We
found neither gold nor much opportunity.

Carving out a life in South Texas is nearly impossible when you don't
speak English, have no practical skills, and have no money. My parents,
neither of whom had ever done manual labor, now worked at it: My
father earned 55 cents per hour lifting boxes; my mom did something
similar for 45 cents per hour. Within a week of our arrival, I was
enrolled in school and my parents were told that I had five months to
learn enough English to keep pace; otherwise, I would be put back a
grade. I became a product of early bilingual education. My English
training would consist of the following: During class, the teacher would
stop her lesson, hold up something, pronounce its name, and point at
me. Then I had to repeat what she said. Then all my classmates would
laugh at me. I learned fast. In five months I was relatively fluent and had
learned to hate both the teacher and the other kids in the class. And to
this day, I can't speak a language unless I speak it fluently. But I did learn
fast, and I spoke English with a fine South Texas twang.

My parents learned as well. They learned that for people in their
forties, English is a very difficult language to master. They learned that
people in Texas ridiculed foreign accents and thought that immigrants
were stupid and uncultured. They learned that working ten to twelve
hours a day at the wages they were earning would kill them. And they
learned that they had to get out of Texas.

We learned as well about segregation in the South. I had no African
American or Hispanic classmates. Even in our very poor neighborhood
there were no families of color. One hot day my father and I were
walking across the park. We walked up to two drinking fountains. They
were both made of white porcelain. Above one a sign read "Whites
Only"; above the other, "Colored Only." "What do the signs say?" my
father asked me. I translated for him. He looked at the white porcelain
drinking fountain labeled "colored" and shook his head: "This is a
strange country. Everyone can tell that this drinking fountain is white,
not colored." Then we learned what the sign meant and we had our first
case of culture shock. It's not the case that Hungarians are a people free
of bigotry; they have their fair share of hatreds toward other groups. It's
that we expected none of it in America. In Hungary we were told

incessantly by the official Communist media of exploitation and segregation in America. But America was supposed to be the closest thing to paradise, and we dismissed all of "that" as pure propaganda in the cold war between East and West. Now, we were coming face-to-face with the reality of both segregation and poverty in our newly adopted country. We wondered what other surprises were waiting for us.

Perhaps it was just Texas, we thought, and most European immigrants don't start their new lives there. My parents saved virtually every penny they made. We were hungry more often than not, but we were rewriting our destiny—we decided to go back to New York. After nine months of hard work, we had saved enough money to buy a car. We locked all of our possessions in the trunk and made the journey back east. As we crossed the George Washington Bridge to the Bronx, the car died, but we were back in New York, ready to start again.

SURVIVING IN NEW YORK

New York City is an amazing place. It is not so much a city as a global metropolis. No fewer than 100 self-contained countries exist side by side, where people can—if they wish—keep their own cultures, speak their own language, and still try to take advantage of what America has to offer. We didn't do that. My parents were mindful that if we decided to live in Little Hungary, I would become a little Hungarian, and the very purpose of their coming to America would be destroyed. So we settled in the South Bronx.

New York City has distinct advantages for urban European immigrants. For one, no one can discriminate against you for speaking English badly, or for speaking with an accent. Most people in New York speak like that. For another, the sheer diversity in the city allows immigrants to find something familiar in the midst of the unfamiliar. Culture shock is thus minimized. Just as important, poverty is not an exceptional, ridiculed condition. Enough people have risen from poverty in New York that the city's residents don't automatically equate poverty with inferiority. And then there was the school system: Even though we lived in a very poor neighborhood, the public schools were so superior to the ones in Texas that my parents felt comfortable about my education.

At the same time, life in New York is brutal and tough. The apartment we found in the Bronx was cheap ($45 per month), but it and the neighborhood around it were in terrible condition. The elevator never worked, and the six flights of stairs took their toll on my parents. We had our own allotment of cockroaches and were forbidden to spray bug killer (it would disturb the quota for each apartment, and lead to "roach wars" between neighbors). Gangs were on every street corner, and kids learned that venturing outside the protection of turf-based gangs meant getting beaten up on most days. My best friend and I were chased home daily by the Chin gang. Prostitution and drug selling (marijuana mostly, and by today's standards small-time) were not uncommon after-school practices for thirteen-year-old children. Cops, typically from outside of the neighborhood, were seen as an invading alien army and were treated with contempt and fear; they, in turn, were constantly abused by teenagers who planted lit cherry bombs in trash cans, timed to explode as the beat cop came around the corner.

My parents did what most immigrants do. They tried desperately to find a niche, to look for opportunity, and to make sure that their child stayed out of trouble and did well in school. There was no problem on the last issue. Our family had mastered the art of guilt. I was reminded daily—both by my parents' condition and by their words—that all the misery we were enduring was for me. If I didn't succeed in school, all their hardship would be wasted and it would be my fault. I became an outstanding student.

My father started to die. He was diagnosed with myasthenia gravis, which at the time was a crippling disease, working on the muscles of the body. On bad days he could not lift his arms above his head; sometimes he couldn't comb his hair. The disease impacted his taste buds. Everything tasted bitter to him (except for banana splits, and this was a great mystery to all of us), and he lost most of his body weight. He was told to stop doing physical labor. Sure! He never *wanted* to do physical labor, but what else could he do? He was a businessman all his life. When he didn't have capital, he would secure it. When he didn't have a business, he would create it. It was all done with intelligence, insight, and a golden gift: He could always convince people to trust him and his ability to make something of nothing. All this required fluency in a language, and that he didn't have in America. English came to him grudgingly, word by word, with phrases and sentences jumbled and unclear. His accent was a thick cross between German and Hungarian. It took patience to understand him, and in New York virtually no one had patience.

So, my dad continued to do hard, manual labor. The pay in New York was better than in Texas, but the conditions were more grueling. He would work ten hours a day and commute (by subway and walking) for three hours a day. After work all he could do at home was to sit and think about his old life and rack his brain about alternatives in his new one. He grew increasingly bitter and alienated.

My mom needed a job as well. The skills she had used in Europe, like my dad's skills, were useless in America. What did she know? One day she decided that there was an area where she had knowledge. In Hungary she would get her hair and nails done weekly. How difficult could it be to go from customer to provider? She would become a beautician. She worked the rounds of beauty salons in Manhattan, but few wanted someone who knew neither hair cutting nor manicuring. Then, one day, persisting, she walked into a shop run by Italians and began to speak with them in fluent Italian. She was adopted immediately, taught the basic elements of the trade, and within months started to do manicures. Eventually she graduated to hair styling. The shop was not a fancy one. Customers paid little and the help got even less. But her pay complemented my dad's wages, and we were surviving.

My parents were not blind, merely caught in savage circumstances. They knew that they could do little else but survive. Eventually, my father would die of hard labor. They saw as well that their son needed another environment in which to grow. The high school I was destined to attend was a breeding ground for felons and murderers, and they would not run the risk that I would become either a killer or a victim. They needed a new, better life.

They did the only thing they could do: They worked longer hours and saved everything. We had meat once a week. I went to the movies five times in the four and a half years we lived in the city. My parents didn't go a single time. They bought me clothes, but I don't ever remember my father buying clothes for himself. Apart from cooking our meals, their non-working, non-sleeping hours consisted of one of five pursuits: going for walks; window-shopping; playing card games with friends; fighting with each other with the bitterness that comes from abject poverty and fading hope; and after what seemed an interminably long time for me, they bought a black-and-white television and watched it, embarrassed and frustrated that their lives were nothing like what was on the little screen.

They began to save money, bit by bit, dollar by dollar. After two years of saving everything, they were ready to move. Then tragedy struck: My father's health collapsed; he was hospitalized and had major surgery. The doctors were great, the low odds of survival were overcome, and my father eventually walked out of the hospital. But we had no health insurance and every penny we had saved was swept away by medical necessity. It meant starting again.

Understandably, my father started to drown in a cesspool of bitterness. Evenings, he would rage about a "country where health care is a luxury. In Hungary we weren't free, but we didn't need to be rich to stay alive!" As my mom worked harder and tried to take care of the family necessities at the same time, my dad's sense of worth gradually disappeared. His recriminations about his new country got more and more vindictive until he and my mom would yell constantly at each other on those nights when they had strength left for verbal battle. And yet, each day my dad would carry around his shrinking, fragile body, looking for any type of work. Fortunately, my mother now started to get tips along with her wages, and between them they began to save again. For three more years they saved until they had built a little nest egg. And then came a time when they knew that they could not stay another day in the city. The nest egg had to do. My father bought a used car and came home and said: "It's time to leave New York. It's time we moved to America now."

THE REST OF AMERICA

The place we moved to really was America: the Midwest. It is not the land of strong spices and not the land of exotic accents. Grand Rapids, Michigan, was the true all-American city. We knew this to be a fact because it was officially designated an All American City by a national organization that creates this designation for cities that are not like New York.

We picked the city in part because we heard that it had a very strong Dutch influence. My mother had lived in Holland, had loved the Dutch, and had admired their tolerance, hard work, and honesty. My parents thought that we could have it both ways: be in America, work hard and succeed, and still enjoy a bit of European influence. Of course, this was not to be. The Dutch that settled western Michigan were not the same Dutch my mom knew before the eve of the Second World War. The people who lived in Grand Rapids had long ago stopped being Europeans; they thought my parents' accents were strange and foreign and wanted to know what these foreigners were doing in their town, and with a son (wearing a leather jacket) who had this very strong Bronx dialect.

Trying to make a living, that's what! My father's health was worse now. He could no longer do any manual labor. His body weight had shrunk dramatically from the 225 pounds he had carried to America; he had lost 100 pounds of it by the time we arrived in Michigan.

While I went off to high school, my parents took their meager savings and opened a *business*: a beauty salon. It was a two-person operation. My father took care of the accounts and money. My mother washed and shampooed, colored hair and permed it, and manicured women's nails. We would rejoice at night when someone made an appointment for a perm. It meant that we could eat, make the rent on the business, and hope for another day.

But we were out of New York, and my parents had a business—and my father believed that if he was smart enough, he would think of an idea that would create a better opportunity for my mom and me before he died and left us. And more important to them, I was becoming an American. My Bronx accent faded, and that flat midwestern dialect became my access to the world. School was easy, my grades were excellent, and I found expression in public speaking, theater, and writing.

At first, the adjustment was not easy. I believed that to be an American, I would have to act like an American. What did American boys do? They played football. I went out for football. I got beaten up at practice, came home bruised, ate vast amounts of food, went back to practice, got beaten up again, and as a defensive end, never ever sacked the quarterback. I gave up football for baseball, the true American game. I decided to be a catcher—that's where most of the action is in baseball. Unfortunately, we had to bring our own gloves, and since we were very poor, I bought a very cheap glove. Our pitcher eventually got a tryout in the majors; he had an excellent fastball. The first one I caught was my last one. His first pitch broke a bone in my hand and I quit baseball.

Clearly, the answer to how one becomes an American had to be something other than sports—or being of Dutch extraction. The most popular kids were Dutch: blond, blue-eyed, and members of the Dutch Christian Reformed Church. I had blue eyes, but everything else was wrong. I wasn't Dutch Christian, I had a long, hooked nose, and my hair was brown and curly—plus, my parents were foreigners. I was condemned to the "outsider" bin along with the Catholics, Jews, blacks, and hippies. Much to my surprise, I discovered that these were also Americans, often more fascinating than the insiders, and if I couldn't belong to the in-group, then at least I could become an "outsider" like them.

Slowly I learned that "outsiders" were at least as American as "insiders." That knowledge was liberating. At home, I defended *everything* in America against my father's tirades and anger. At school I would write papers and articles about discrimination and poverty, and freedom of speech. I read everything Steinbeck wrote and used great passages in oratorical contests (contests that I began to win). The American Legion (is there something more American than the American Legion?) awarded me second prize in their annual oratorical contest, and while I burned with anger about not getting first place, my mom still treasures the little statue I brought home so many years ago.

This was the prize for my parents. Their son was making it in America. He was becoming an American and he was going to have opportunity. While they continued to struggle financially (their annual income hovered around $3,000 a year) and with health problems (my father was now talking regularly about dying), they focused single-mindedly on their great decision: that perhaps they were right all along in coming to America.

A thousand times they would tell me that I had only one job: to get into college. Their circumstances had never allowed them the opportunity for appropriate schooling. My father dropped out of the seventh grade to take care of his mother and sister; my mom did likewise before she could graduate from the ninth grade. They refused to allow me to get part-time jobs; anything that would increase the possibility of my dropping out of school would have meant that all their suffering was wasted. Guilt continued as my stimulus to excel.

In my senior year, I was offered a number of scholarships to college. These were National Defense Education Act (NDEA) scholarships, provided by the federal government for outstanding students in need.

Complemented by NDEA loans, they afforded me the college of my choice, and an unlimited future.

I left Grand Rapids, graduated from Oakland University, and with another round of NDEA fellowships, went on to graduate school at the University of Minnesota. And my father, desperate to secure a stable future for my mother before he would die, had an idea. One day, walking around downtown, deep in thought, he glanced at a wig shop. They were selling "Italian, human hair" wigs for $400. He rushed home, called me, and asked me to write a letter to a manufacturer of wigs in Taiwan. Three months later, my parents opened a wig shop, selling "Italian, handmade wigs" for $99. In one year, their income went from $3,000 to $115,000. My father, now very ill and having shrunk to 110 pounds, talked my mom into going back to Hungary on vacation (it was their first vacation since arriving in America). They spent two wonderful weeks in Budapest. At the end, he said to her: "Edit, I don't like this place. I've become an American, whether or not I like it. Let's go home." They came back, visited me at graduate school, flew back to Michigan, bought their first brand-new car, and then my dad died.

My father struggled, worked, succeeded, and died in a span of thirteen years in America. He became an American just before he passed away, and he came to believe that his sacrifices were not wasted. I owe him and my mom every opportunity I have had in life. At the same time, their struggles have helped to frame my outlook on life: a great love of this country tempered by the knowledge of its imperfections, buoyed by the potential of what it can become. My parents' struggles taught me as well about the importance of politics in our social and economic lives. Our lives were not driven by vague, mystical, unintelligible, or even natural forces. It was politics and national policies that determined the type of economy where hardworking men and women struggled to survive on a pittance of wages. There were national health-care policies that withheld the quality of health care my father needed to live past the age of sixty-one or to have a life without constant physical suffering. But there was also a national immigration policy that allowed us to come to this country in the first place, and an educational policy that allowed me to go to college and graduate school. And it was the same economic policy that helped to frame our poverty that also gave my father the opportunity to fashion something else at the end. Political decisions brought us here, made life so very difficult for us, and gave me my chance to become a productive citizen. I learned that politics makes an enormous difference in our lives and that politics is not neutral. It is not something you can either take an interest in or ignore. Eventually it will help or harm you, or both. I learned that ignoring it simply ignores a driving force in our lives.

My parents never understood about American politics. They loved Jack Kennedy and feared Lyndon Johnson (he was a Texan, after all). They had not the vaguest idea about their senators or member of Congress. They believed that the Immigration and Naturalization Service (INS) watched every step they took until they became citizens, and even then they wondered if the INS could strip them of their citizenship if they jaywalked or got parking tickets. They voted in every election because citizens were supposed to vote, and they voted Democratic because that was the party their son liked.

They never made the linkage between their lives and what politicians actually did in office. Nor did they ever think that there was anything they, as citizens, could do about what government was doing to them through the passage of public policies. They were socialized into a different political world. The world of democracy was as alien to them as their adopted society. They and their families before them grew up in political systems in which they played little or no role. The Communist government ruled by fear; fascist and monarchist governments before it had paid little attention to the desires of most citizens. Government and politics were only forces of harm and pain to my parents. Their approach was to ignore these forces as much as possible.

In this, I could not convince them otherwise. Once my parents actually earned enough money to pay taxes, they would rage at the unfairness of giving money to the government. "It only encourages them," my father would say. Or, "If they would use it for decent health care, then it would be worth it!" He had absolutely no sense that there was anything he or I, or most citizens, could do about these things. They thought it childish and myopic that I had a sense of optimism about shaping and forming the contours of the political world. They thought it silly when I said that they were either part of the problem or part of the solution. Government and politics were overwhelming, gigantic forces and smart people stayed out of the way. They hoped that I would not waste any of my time being involved with such foolishness.

GROWING UP AND GETTING INVOLVED

My parents taught me the importance of both education and politics. The first they did with the sheer power of the sacrifices they made for me. I learned of the importance of politics by observing their lives and coming to understand the connections to the political forces shaping them. And so, without necessarily understanding all of this, I moved toward the twin worlds of education and politics.

I married my college sweetheart. Together we ventured out to graduate school with a game plan. She would support us while I got my Ph.D. and then I would do likewise—my degree in political science, hers in psychology. Buried under the abysmal cold and snow of Minnesota, I learned to become a political scientist, an occupation totally alien to my parents. All they knew about this "business" was that I was succeeding and their son would be a "doctor," certainly the first doctor in their family.

My first job out of graduate school took me to Tucson and the University of Arizona. My new colleagues recruited me in the wintertime, a season of paradise there. I went back home to dreary snow showers and convinced my wife that our destiny was out west. How American!

And so we came to the place that is the new America. The Southwest has witnessed the last great migration of a people constantly on the move. Even today, roughly 20 percent of all Americans move from their place of residence to another, the ultimate manifestation of hope and optimism that something better is just around the corner. Many come to the Southwest, and of those who do, most fall in love and stay.

We fell in love and stayed. The university turned out to be a magic place. It allowed me to teach and to learn. The work—unlike popular conceptions of it—is complicated and time-consuming. But there is nothing more exciting than opening up new worlds to students and getting them excited about the learning process. In turn, a teacher is worthless if she or he doesn't explore the boundaries of knowledge and help to shape the knowledge base from which all teaching occurs. We call it research, and it is a wondrous world of discovery and creation.

In exchange, we are paid well; never enough to become rich, never enough to reach the highest quality of life, but much better than most Americans.

Most people would settle for a great job with good pay and enormous emotional rewards. But the American dream is even more expansive. It offers the promise of endless possibilities for some who work hard enough and are lucky as well. We found not only university life but also a community to which we could belong.

It is not true that America is a rootless nation. In the great old cities of New York, Chicago, Boston, and San Francisco, old social and political structures exist that are nearly impossible to penetrate by most ordinary people. Sometimes older structures are replaced by newer ones, such as the transformations that shifted politics from white to black hands in the cities of Detroit and Atlanta. But too often these communities are still controlled by entrenched economic and social elites that have always governed the lives of their cities.

This is not true in the Southwest. Here, the established social power of the older families is constantly swept over by waves of newcomers who are restless and hungry for a new life and passionate about their new surroundings. Here, the badge of distinction is not your historical standing and your network of social affiliations but your desire to be a citizen of your new community. Newcomers who have lived here for more than three years are called "natives." Here, we are all immigrants: people who have fled from other parts of the nation and the world, trying to create a new life for ourselves.

It is possible in the Southwest—with sufficient willpower and commitment of time—to shape and fashion your community. Entrance into the political process is wide open to those who have the dedication and the energy. After only five years of living in Tucson, and disenchanted with the direction of the community, I ran for office and won a seat on the city council. Within the next ten years, I became the mayor of the thirtieth largest city in the United States. My mother thought that this was a great tragedy that had fallen on the family. In her view, government was bad, and good politicians would all be assassinated. She feared constantly for her son. She would often say: "You work too hard. Don't you want to enjoy life? Aren't you tired of this political nonsense?" My father didn't live long enough to see his immigrant son come to govern a major American city.

Looking at the course of my life is both a bit overwhelming and deceptive. Only in America could an immigrant child come to find his place and be so easily accepted not only into the fabric of society but also into its ranks of governors. My activism had led me to a central place in the workings of the National League of Cities and the U.S. Conference of Mayors. Often I testified before both houses of Congress on fundamental policy problems and legislation. I conferred inside the White House on subjects vital to my city. Since leaving office, I've worked through nonprofit groups and agencies of the U.S. government, training mayors and governors and presidential personnel in dozens of nations rising from the ashes of the former Soviet empire. And in an ironic twist, I was part of the international delegation that observed and legitimized Hungary's first democratic elections after the collapse of the Iron Curtain. Meanwhile, I've taken enormous pride and pleasure in the thousands of graduate and undergraduate students who have worked and studied with me.

For me, the American dream has become a reality. I am a respected member of my community. I live in a house that is modest by some standards yet one that my parents would never have dreamed of owning. I'm not rich, but I will never go hungry, will never have to worry about finding a decent job, will never spend sleepless nights worrying about the future of my family.

Yet my story is a dangerous one. It is possible to assume in its reading that we can all make it and that the rainbow of success is reachable for all of us who have the dedication and desire to make it happen. I was endowed with a family that sacrificed everything for me. Yet even that would not have been enough. They often made decisions that didn't work and at times made decisions that did work, but they didn't know how or why. Like them, I made a series of decisions and came to forks in the road and took them blindly, not knowing the consequences of my actions. In short, I was very lucky. I know that luck without hard work would not have been enough. But without luck, neither would I have succeeded, nor would my parents have achieved their goals.

Many, perhaps most, immigrants have not made it; the best they can do is to survive. Many of the kids I grew up with in New York had parents no different and dreams no less driving than mine. Some of them are now in prison; some of them are dead of drugs and gang violence. Others struggle at dead-end jobs, seeing no future for themselves or their children. The immigrants in Tucson, legal and illegal alike, are some of the hardest-working people I've met. But their opportunities are so limited that luck and desire are overwhelmed by their deepening poverty.

And what of the native born? Most middle- and low-income Americans, expecting and working for a continued bettering of their lives, have seen a steady decline in their incomes over the last two decades. The American dream of opportunity has slipped from millions who find themselves in dead-end jobs with low pay and arduous working conditions, and with no benefits or health insurance. Tens of millions more are struggling to hold on to what they have. They work longer hours than ever before, and their spouses work as well. Roughly two out of three children today are growing up in families where no parent is home in the daytime. They are out working, struggling to survive.

There are, and have always been, two faces to America. The one face is of great dreams realized: people who can and do "make it" in American society. There are countless stories of children and parents fighting and achieving wealth, fame, glory, and happiness. There is the other face as well: many millions of Americans who struggle just as hard but don't make it, lose the shape and form of the American dream, and die from overwork and a loss of hope. No other wealthy country offers such opposites. In modern European democracies, the promise is that people will not starve and they will not die of inadequate health care, food, or housing, and a decent educational system is guaranteed. The quality of life of most people in Western Europe will rise and fall in tandem, and mostly those families who have always been on top of the pyramid will be able to offer their children dreams limited only by their desires. But there is no promise there of a dream of untold success from any stratum of society.

In America, life can be and is both bountifully rich *and* cruel. The vast resources of our country guarantee an incredible diversity of opportunity. Individual initiative and luck are powerful bridges to success. Yet real access to education and opportunity is fashioned in critical ways by politics, government, and public policies. Public policies determine to a very great extent who wins and who loses, who is helped and who is not. They do so by making an enormous difference in creating access to opportunity and in helping to decide how cruel or fortunate life becomes.

I would not have made it without some of those policies, and my parents could have made it if there had been better policies. Today, the struggling mother with a young child can dream and work as hard as she can and get nowhere if the jobs available do not pay a decent wage and if she can't get decent, affordable child care. In turn, wages, job creation, and affordable health care are powerfully affected not only by market forces but also by government policies favoring one approach to opportunity over another.

In these and many other ways, politics and public policy impact on every aspect of our lives. The water we drink, the air we breathe, the roads we travel (or can't), the education of our children, the ability to harness new technologies, the physical safety and security of our society, and basic issues of fairness and justice are all impacted by government and public policies. In fact, reducing the impact of politics—fashionable among conservative policy makers and critics—would not have a uniform effect. It would impact critically on the availability of opportunity for people in America, bringing more freedom for some and less access to the resources of America for many more.

POLITICS IN AMERICA

Politics matters, and America is blessed with democratic politics. Democratic politics means that the ultimate judgment for "how it's working" is left to those who are affected by it. Unlike my parents' experience with politics, who governs, and how, are ultimately decided not by impersonal forces, coercion, or hereditary authority but by voters. It is their right to guess wrong and their right to correct their mistakes. We have in our country not only social and economic opportunity but political opportunity as well.

Political opportunity is important, however, only if we care to use it, and fewer of us care to do so every year. Tens of millions have chosen not to make the judgment. Tens of millions have grown so alienated from the political process that they think it a waste of time to cast a ballot. Most Americans no longer trust government, and they are beginning to believe, like my parents did, that these impersonal forces provide little but bad news in their lives.

Democracy cannot function this way. If people lose faith in the governors they select and in the institutions they have permitted to govern them, democracy will wither and die. Yet in the entire history of humanity's experimentation with different forms of governance, no one has found a better alternative than democratic politics.

Like most things about the United States, American democracy is unique among its peers. We rely more than any other democracy on the judgments of individual citizens to make democracy work because we lack strong ideologies, ideologically motivated political parties, and large-scale social movements. Our institutions represent many hybrids, compromises, and complexities. The political relationships among the various institutions of the federal government, and the relationships between the federal government, the states, and the cities, after two hundred years of evolution and experimentation, impose difficult burdens on both policy makers and voters. Voters especially, in order to fulfill their responsibilities in a democratic society, must navigate through a bewildering maze of complexity to understand what government is doing and whether their representatives are fulfilling the promises they made to get into office.

Yet if they fail, democracy fails. If they make consistently wrong decisions, democracy will lurch from failure to failure, until failure will destroy it. If they withdraw from judgment and do not participate in the act of voting, democracy will be captured by a small minority that will steer government mostly for its own benefit. Ultimately, that outcome will destroy it as well.

I learned in office that voters are far more responsible about their citizenship roles than we suspect. At the same time, they know far too little about politics, government, and public policies. It's not that they don't know who their senators or representatives are, or what laws were passed in Congress last week. These they can learn quickly and in time to make judgments. What they lack is *empathy*: a basic understanding of what their elected officials do, how they do it, and why. The absence of this knowledge is far more serious. It is the key in today's society for making appropriate judgments by citizens about the great experiments being conducted around their well-being and the future of society. Without this knowledge, they cannot fulfill their responsibilities as voters, and if they cannot fulfill their responsibilities, then democracy is surely doomed.

Many social critics place the blame squarely on the shoulders of citizens, arguing that they have failed to pay attention and to remain knowledgeable. This charge is unfair. The civics lessons we learn are meager preparation for understanding the complexities of the political process. Citizens have ample information available about some aspects of governance from a very diverse set of sources, but the most easily absorbed mechanisms of information—television and radio—grossly oversimplify political events. Meanwhile, desperately hunting for economic survival, most family members have little time to spend with one another. No wonder that they spend virtually no time searching for information about politics and government above and beyond exposure to the most available media.

Politicians have not worked very hard to bridge the empathy/ knowledge gap. It is often easier for them, and politically safer, to climb on the bandwagon of simplification, denunciation, and ridicule. Inadvertently, they add to the cycle of distrust and deteriorating political culture in society.

I learned in office that most citizens, despite their very high evaluations of me, had virtually no knowledge of what I did, how I did it, or what motivated me to act. More critically, the media and other politicians were constantly bombarding them with such simplistic and distorted images of political behavior that most citizens couldn't avoid the impression that the system was falling apart and that politicians were, by and large, liars, crooks, and cheats. On the rare occasions when we could talk about the political process, and on the rarer occasions when a few citizens could actually observe firsthand the behavior of their representatives, they would inevitably express great surprise at the variance between reality and the images to which they were exposed.

If American democracy is to survive intact, we need to have more of these conversations and less of the rhetoric of simplistic denunciation. Citizens deserve the right to make judgments about their government and their representatives in the context of an empathetic view of what goes on inside the political laboratory. Otherwise, we will lose the essence of democracy: that governmental performance is to be guided by the wishes of the people. If citizens continue to lose their perspective, this nation of great opportunity will become so for only the few and the very lucky. And then the rare immigrant stories will remain just that: rare.

2

Democracy in America

"Politics comes from two words: one is the Greek word *poli,* which means many, and the other word is *ticks,* which means blood sucking insects."[1]

The end of the cold war came suddenly, and with it came the triumph of democracy and free-market capitalism. Why did the West emerge victorious? The most seductive explanation for the end of the Communist system is the one based on the superiority of democratic politics and free-market economics. The East failed because it could not continue to compete against the inherent superiority of these forces in the postindustrial world. Ultimately, three interrelated factors are supposed to have precipitated the fall of the Soviet empire. First, Communist governments were unable to create public policies capable of successfully addressing economic and social problems. Second, a declining standard of living reinforced belief in the incompetence of governors. Finally, the system lost legitimacy and credibility in the eyes of critical segments of society.

So we won. Communism didn't bury us. Instead, capitalists and democrats stand on the ashes of the Soviet Union, still awed at the speed of its collapse. Nor is the trend toward democracy confined to Communist states alone. Over the last two hundred years the number of democracies in the world grew from three to sixty-one. Over the last twenty years, the number of democracies doubled worldwide. In countries as disparate as Cambodia, Haiti, and Nigeria, civic groups are struggling to plant the seeds of democracy, often with outside assistance. While there are exceptions to the trend, the direction of history is presently unmistakable.

Or is it? If democracy has triumphed, why are people in the more-established democracies showing such signs of wear and tear? If this is the end of history, why are the victors so tired? The sense of triumph that greeted the end of the cold war should have infused the Western democracies with energy and a great feeling of optimism. Instead, pessimism, frustration, and a sense of impending failure seem to rule the day.

The Lombardi League in Italy, Jean-Marie Le Pen's movement in France, and the upsurge of neo-Nazi movements in Germany and elsewhere in Europe represent clear signs of growing intolerance in the heart of Western European democracies. Support for governing majorities is shrinking or disappearing in most Western European states, from Britain in the west to Austria in the east.

The situation is no better in North America. Canadians are fed up with their government. In the United States, only a quarter of the American public has anything positive to say about Congress or the federal government. The office of the presidency, usually held in high esteem, is taking a similar beating and has done so increasingly over the last three decades. In the 1950s, it took President Dwight D. Eisenhower five years before his "honeymoon" with the American public ended. In the 1990s, President Clinton's honeymoon ended in the third month of his presidency.

Nearly all aspects of government are viewed with great pessimism by the American public, and the pessimism is increasing; more than twice as many people today, compared to thirty years ago, believe that the government does not serve their interests. Few Americans today are willing to say that the government is doing a good job in dealing with critical national issues. No wonder, then, that few others besides used-car salespeople and lawyers are held in lower esteem than those who run for office and claim to represent the public. Holding office or being a government employee in our democracy is now seen as a dishonorable profession.

The credibility and legitimacy of our political institutions and the men and women who run them are judged negatively by more citizens today than at any other time in the last hundred years. If it is true that the Soviet empire collapsed ultimately over a loss of legitimacy among those who governed, then we may be in trouble as well.

One point is certain: We are indeed a troubled nation. Proposals for structural changes—constitutional amendments to balance budgets, term limits for elected officials, ideas to fundamentally restructure the role of money and special interests in campaigns—reflect deep-seated worries that our institutions and the broader political processes driving them no longer work. These proposals also stem from the persistent belief that the people who represent us and drive the machinery of government are doing a lousy job and that the ones waiting in the wings to replace them will not do any better. Can democracy survive when we no longer seem to like what it's doing to us?

DEMOCRACY IN AMERICA

Why do democracies survive and flourish? One school of thought argues that democracies are anchored to high living standards and economic policies that promote a strong and large middle class. Another sees the survivability of democracies as anchored in a culture that is supportive of democratic governance, with feelings of positive affect for democracy, beliefs about being able to influence the course of political affairs, and attitudes of trust toward other citizens. A third view argues that the key to the survival of democracies lies in the robustness of mediating institutions—some political, some social—that regularly teach habits of participation, a sense of community, and tolerance for long-term problem solving, qualities necessary for the maintenance of democratic governance.

Of course, democracies cannot survive for long if their methods of governance fail to produce decent policies. If governments cannot address vital societal issues even after one set of leaders is replaced by another, then people will grow wary and may search for nondemocratic solutions to their concerns. When dramatic changes affect the economic well-being of large numbers of citizens, democracy can be jeopardized if leaders fail to find ways of relieving economic stresses. Yet recent history teaches us that stable democracies such as the United States and Great Britain are able to survive even disastrous economic times. We survived the storms of economic despair during the Great Depression without chucking away our democratic institutions.

Neither is the ultimate threat to democracy the short-term failure of public policies outside the economic realm. Plenty of historical examples exist of major policy mistakes that failed to address enormous societal problems. Eventually, these failures led to fundamental policy changes without destroying our democratic political processes. Banning alcohol in the 1920s created organized crime and warfare on our streets and we survived—not through martial law but by changing our public policies. Decades of legal segregation and the denial of equal opportunity for minorities and women in virtually all aspects of life ultimately led to massive policy changes that are still evolving today. Despite outbreaks of violence and resistance by state and local authorities, these changes were accomplished through existing institutional structures. Enormous conflicts over Vietnam escalated into violence and civil disobedience, yet we muddled through failed policies. Our democratic institutions even survived the incarceration of innocent Asian citizens during World War II, the anticommunist witch-hunts of the 1950s, and J. Edgar Hoover's abuses of civil liberties as head of the FBI.

Emerging democracies may not survive for long under the onslaught of declining economic circumstances or failed public policies. The ultimate threat to *stable* democracies, however, is more likely to come when the credibility and legitimacy of the system are in doubt. When the civic culture and the mediating institutions that reinforce it are no longer strong enough to withstand policy failures and declining economic circumstances, then democratic governance is in trouble. Democratic institutions are in jeopardy when large numbers of citizens no longer believe that their representatives work for them, or when tolerance and trust disappear from the political culture and citizens come to feel that their participation no longer matters.

American democracy is based on a constitution and historical events that make our form of government rather unique. Irrespective of how our civics textbooks portray it, the American Revolution was born without political philosophy, without a coherent ideology, and without a nationalist spirit. The Declaration of Independence is a pragmatic document, identifying specific grievances against the English, and without much theory about how a new democracy should operate. Even Thomas Jefferson, considered to be the leading philosopher of the period, showed little interest in political theory or abstract thinking about the nature of government in the letters he wrote to close associates and friends. Instead, his letters focus on quite provincial matters and concentrate on specific legal problems and specific policies. In a similar vein, the Constitution is a document created "by compromise on details rather than by agreement on a theory."[2] Our political system was built by people who were on the edge of a new and unexplored frontier and had to address a series of pragmatic problems about their future. They established a democratic government based on *experimentation* and *flexibility* through a series of checks and balances designed to minimize the concentration of governmental power and to allow both governments and individuals to maximize experimentation with ideas and policies.

The founders of our nation handed down to us a democratic process that is meant to work the same way as a scientist works in a laboratory. The scientific method is, in contrast to ideological approaches to politics, one of experimentation and testing. The scientist puts on a lab coat, enters the laboratory, and, based on the best competing explanations about the physical world, begins to experiment with different combinations of formulas, with the objective of reaching a desired outcome. When that outcome occurs, she knows that she has succeeded, and until proven wrong through the same process of experimentation, she now has an answer to her problem.

Unlike many other democracies—where the political process is driven by institutionalized ideological conflict—American democracy was designed to function pragmatically as a political laboratory. Voters decide ultimately which people will wear the lab coats. Those voted into the laboratory in turn hire others to help them with the experiments. We elect the key people in the laboratory because we believe them to be the best scientists available for the job. This is so because during campaigns they agree to pursue projects we believe need to be addressed and they tell us that they have ways of conducting the experiments successfully. Separation of powers and checks and balances in the political laboratory serve to create a diversity of perspectives about appropriate methods for conducting the experiments and a diversity of views for evaluating the outcomes of the experiments. Likewise, decentralization of power in America allows for the creation of thousands of laboratories. Fifty states and 15,000 cities work on similar and overlapping problems. We elect more than a half million people who don lab coats and experiment with public policies. Experiments in health care, transportation, education, and economic development provide a rich array of choices to be emulated, avoided, or modified at the federal, regional, and local levels.

And who is to judge if an experiment is successful? Unlike the scientific process, that judgment is left to the public. The people in the lab coats are required (through open meetings and various "sunshine" laws) to reveal and debate their experiments in public. We make a collective decision when we vote about whether to continue the experiments or to get new people to don the lab coats and try again. The Bill of Rights and other constitutional protections for individual liberties allow us the freedom to look at the evidence from the laboratory, to discuss and debate the results, and to try to rally others around our evaluations. A vibrant political opposition and a free press are crucial for this effort, providing (in principle) enough information for citizens to judge critically the effects of the experiment.

At least, that is how the system is meant to function, but this democracy-by-experimentation is not an easy one to sustain. It requires far more attention and deliberation from voters than in majoritarian democracies where parliamentary systems reign. In many other democracies, parliamentary systems are coupled to relatively cohesive and disciplined parties. This linkage eliminates for voters the confusion felt by citizens in the United States when their representatives break ranks across party lines, vote against their own parties, and denounce their own leaders. This great fluidity at the national level is accompanied by a cacophony from state and local leaders who also dispute their parties and the direction of the national experiments.

Even if we are attentive and caring, making rational citizen judgments about the success of political experiments is an arduous and difficult process for most of us. It seems at times chaotic and at times wasteful as experiments are changed or abandoned or duplicated across a number of governmental settings. At times the experiments are bound to fail when the laboratory doesn't have enough resources to make them successful, irrespective of the efforts of the people in the laboratory. On occasion, a few people in the lab coats will actually abscond with equipment (fraud), spill precious resources (waste), or even abuse the equipment (Watergate) in order to keep their jobs. Yet as chaotic and difficult as this process seems, it is nevertheless consistent with the experimental orientation of the Founding Fathers.

The most difficult problem for responsible citizens in this political system is to try to determine when there is too much failure in the laboratory. By definition, experiments cannot succeed all the time. It is only by doing experiments, failing, making corrections, and then succeeding that the desired outcome can be reached. In the interim, there are enormous costs for failure. Experiments in the scientific laboratories that have not yet led to a cure for AIDS and cancer have caused untold suffering and death in the lives of millions of citizens. In the political laboratory, the failure to find appropriate answers to the problems of poverty, discrimination, unbalanced economic development, environmental degradation, and inadequate health care has caused abject misery in the lives of millions of Americans as well, and in some instances this failure threatens the well-being of future generations. These experiments are not trivial; their consequences for society are enormous.

The process of experimentation by trial and error requires a citizenry that can evaluate outcomes with tolerance, understanding, and empathy. In our democracy, because we implicitly understand that we know of no *one* right answer to human problems, we agree to tolerate some failures of policy, recognizing that the process is an experimental one. We tolerate some failure as long as we know that we are making progress and that we are doing the best we can. The "scientists" can be booted out when they promise us that their experiments will work and they don't work. We toss them out as well when they promise to run experiments but don't do so, or when they experiment on projects that we feel are not important and constitute a waste of society's resources. If they damage or abuse the laboratory, we will toss them out as well. Electoral punishment for failure in the laboratory is a critical part of the democratic process.

The great threat to an established democracy occurs when public confidence in the laboratory itself has eroded because citizens have come to believe that all of the people in the lab coats—those working in the laboratory and those who wish to replace them—are incompetent or crooked. And distrust is only inflamed further when new people apply for the job of "scientist," promise instant success in the laboratory, and then betray the promises on which they knew they couldn't deliver.

These threats to democracy destroy its main anchor: a sense of civic community. Civic community is made up of a number of ingredients. Partly it consists of a belief that the system will work as long as we keep an eye on the experimenters and, when needed, replace them. Partly it involves a belief that active and considered participation by voters is essential for making the system work and that participation in the political process is a worthwhile investment in society.

We don't know precisely where this civic culture comes from, what causes it, or how fragile it is. In some cases, it may be quite enduring. A strong civic culture is extremely difficult to develop, but once it has taken root, it is far more stable than we may think. It would be foolish and dangerous, though, to think that it will endure without attention and nurturing.

<h2>LOSING EMPATHY AND TOLERANCE</h2>

Civic culture is more than reacting to good or bad government policy performance and more than enjoying a high standard of living. A political culture conducive to experimental democracy needs a citizenry that is tolerant of diversity and occasional failure, is optimistic about the long term, engages the political system and gains gratification from participatory experiences, and has a sense of understanding and empathy toward those who work in the political laboratory.

Of all these aspects of civic culture, the characteristics of trust, understanding, and especially empathy may be most crucial. Unless citizens hold a deep sense of empathy and understanding toward those who experiment with policies, how can they gauge fairly a political system that spends their taxes but is not meeting a number of their critical needs in the short run? Lack of empathy and understanding about what happens in the political process will eventually doom the experimental method of democratic governance. Citizens will come to feel that all of their political "scientists" are liars, crooks, and cheats. In response, the people working in the laboratory will spend less time on experiments and more time publicly denouncing each other and the shortcomings of the laboratory. Long-term experiments will be cut short. Eventually, the only people who will be hired to run the laboratory will be those who pledge to reduce the costs of running it or to close it altogether.

Unfortunately, we are rapidly losing our sense of empathy toward those involved in the process of governance. Fewer of us each year can understand what politicians do, and we grow more critical toward them and toward our institutions of government. Recently, nearly two out of three people surveyed disagreed with the statement that people in government were doing their best in a difficult job. More worrisome was the finding that 60 percent indicated dissatisfaction with the way democracy is working in the United States. Contrast these results with earlier decades. In 1931, the position of politician was ranked as the sixth most-respected occupation, ahead of college professors and businesspeople. In 1943, U.S. senators and state governors were ranked ahead of all prestigious occupations on the list. As late as 1960, federal officials were ranked very high on honesty and ability and were seen as serving the public.

Part of the reason for our unhappiness with the political system is our perception of government performance. But the failure to remedy society's problems is only part of the reason why empathy and trust are declining. For numerous other reasons, we don't comprehend the circumstance of those who govern us, and we are falling prey to simplistic explanations regarding why things are not working the way we want them to work.

How many of us have any sense of understanding of what a mayor or a legislator or the president of the United States does on a daily basis? Our access to information is greater than at any other time in history. Satellites give us access to an incredible range of national and international news. Over 100,000 new books are published in North America every year. Electronic mail and the Internet give us instant access to information from the comfort of our homes and offices. Yet few if any citizens have much inkling about the daily lives of those who represent us in government.

Americans have never had a love affair with politicians or politics, and we can argue about the extent to which understanding and empathy toward political figures have been higher in the past than today. Mark Twain supposedly said that politicians were America's only native criminal class. Surveys and opinion polls, showing a deterioration of trust and an increase of pessimism over the last few decades, fail to measure directly the extent to which empathy and understanding have declined in the last century. What is important is not how much less empathy exists today compared to the past but that empathy is declining at a time when it is most needed. Why this should be so is due to three new factors on the political landscape that, when combined, make trust and understanding more important today than ever before.

One major change confronting the American political system today revolves around the decline in the role of mediating institutions, especially of political parties. Fewer citizens are ardent partisans, and partisanship has been steadily eroding in the United States. The percentage of voters with positive feelings toward one party and negative feelings toward the other has declined from about half of the electorate in 1952 to about one-third of voters at the turn of the twenty-first century. The percentage of voters feeling neutral toward both parties more than doubled during that time.

These attitudes about political parties are reflected as well in how citizens vote. At the start of the twentieth century, knowing whether a person voted for the Democratic or the Republican candidate for president almost perfectly predicted which candidate the person would vote for in congressional and gubernatorial races. Even in the 1960s, partisan identification strongly affected voting behavior (for example, voters viewed Richard Nixon in a significantly more favorable light than John F. Kennedy, but Nixon could not overcome Democratic loyalties). By the 1980s, there was very little correlation between partisan identification and voting for various national offices. Not surprisingly, Ross Perot—a billionaire who claimed to represent the aspirations of average Americans—ran against both parties in 1992 and despite colossal blunders that cut deeply into his support still captured one in five votes.

As long as a strong sense of party affiliation existed in the political culture, less empathy and understanding were required from citizens. Rooting for and believing in those who represent *our* party can dampen disappointments with policy failures and political setbacks. Partisans dismiss failures on their side as unfortunate and temporary ("They may be bums, but they are our bums"), whereas they see failures by the other party as inevitable ("What can you expect from those guys?"). As party affiliation declines, however, citizens and political officials alike stand before each other more naked than ever.

Their nakedness becomes even more evident when declining partisanship is accompanied by a sense of distance from government, and in fact the decline in partisanship has been paralleled by increasing distance from government. In the 1960s, despite great social and cultural turmoil, only a little over one-third of registered voters believed that government was run by "a few special interests." By the middle of the 1990s, about 80 percent agreed with the statement. How bad are these numbers? In a poll taken in 1993, the citizens of Ukraine—a nation that has no democratic civic culture—responded in the same way to a similar question.

Once parties decline in salience and people begin to feel that government is no longer theirs, the work of citizens in an experimental democracy becomes very difficult. Voters may have to choose among candidates contesting no fewer than 40 different seats in a typical city. Voter information pamphlets—issued as guides for citizens before an election—may provide more than a hundred pages of information just for state offices and ballot measures. To make their workload even more difficult, voters also have to evaluate numerous propositions and referenda on public policies. Absent the reliance on political parties for cues, how can they make good judgments without spending all their time seeking information?

As important as political parties and party affiliation are for the political system, they are by no means the only important aspects of mediating institutions in democracies. Just as salient are the voluntary, nonpolitical organizations and activities that promote a sense of civic culture and increase our trust and empathy toward government and democracy. A strong and consistent involvement with churches, neighborhood groups, and voluntary organizations leads to what scholars have called "civic engagement," promoting norms about trustworthiness, collaboration, and tolerance for long-term political processes. Without such civic engagement, "nearly everyone feels powerless, exploited, and unhappy."[3]

It is, however, all too easy to demonstrate a rather consistent decline in those mediating institutions, institutions that could complement the cues given to voters by political parties. Taking the period between the early 1970s and the 1990s, newspaper reading—indicating attempts to keep in touch with what is happening in one's community—declined by 33 percent. Regular church attendance decreased by 16 percent. Union membership dropped by 44 percent. Nearly 20 percent fewer people were involved with voluntary organizations in the 1990s than was true in the 1970s. Even socializing with neighbors had declined by over 23 percent. The range of mediating institutions historically involved with reinforcing trust and empathy in the civic culture is being used less and less by today's Americans.

In addition to the decline of mediating institutions, a second change has been brought about by the problem of false closeness. This refers to the degree to which the media in general and television in particular seem to have brought the political process closer to the public. There are two C-SPAN channels available to tens of millions of homes with cable services, and CNN has been ranked as the second most popular cable network, available to over 60 million subscribers (C-SPAN has at times reached an audience of over 50 million subscribers). Even traditional news outlets have expanded their coverage of the political processes in response to cable television. At the local level, most large cities have public access channels that televise live all meetings of their city's governing bodies.

Wouldn't this increased media scrutiny lead to greater understanding of government and the political process? Not if it is an artificial closeness: The experimental process is complex and at times ugly. The increased visibility of the political process has shown us mostly the ugly parts of the process, not the complexity. Worse still, the cameras are creating their own effects. Dissidents posture before C-SPAN cameras (often in front of an empty chamber), hurling invective in hopes of attracting the attention of a few voters at home. Debates on the floor of the House of Representatives are captured in 30-second "time bites" on the evening news, designed by the participants as statements more to get *on* the news than to influence fellow members. Even on an issue as fundamentally important and complex as the restructuring of the nation's health-care system, little newspaper ink and television time were spent on explaining to the American public the range of problems and options being faced by the people working on the policy. Instead of giving citizens greater opportunities to see inside the laboratory, they are treated to waves of attacks charging gridlock, ineptitude, wasteful spending, personal gain, and sex scandals.

Increased media exposure has not provided greater understanding of the nature of ongoing policy experiments. Heightened coverage of politics has provided information and commentary but typically without context. Attention by the media has been riveted on those able to drum up the most conflict and the most interesting (that is, conflictual and negative) stories. Greater attention to the political process by the media may actually function to provoke greater distrust and to create a false sense of understanding.

A recent study illustrated the relevance of the media in shaping public attitudes toward the political system and the officials who serve in it.[4] Perceptions of lack of waste in government, presumably gleaned from critical national media attention, were found to be the most salient dimension in accounting for citizen trust in government. In turn, trust in government was strongly related to trust in members of Congress. However, direct contact with members of Congress—creating some degree of empathy toward officials—was the most powerful determinant of citizens' trust in their representatives. Empathy, resulting from direct contact, seems to be very important in shaping citizens' views about political officials. Unfortunately, such studies also show how difficult it is to develop empathy: It is a Herculean task for both citizens and their representatives to stay in direct contact with one another when a congressional district contains more than half a million people and senators must represent millions of citizens. Meanwhile, most citizens are dependent on media that not only fail to create a sense of empathy but also tend to fuel distrust in the political process.

The third change involves the complexity problem. We are aware of this issue in our everyday lives, yet we seldom apply it to democratic governance: We live today in an era of great complexity. Complex problems require complex experiments in the laboratory and complex solutions. Experimenting under conditions of heightened complexity requires more knowledge and greater patience and understanding. Instead, we struggle against complexity. Over forty years of addiction to television has taught us that nearly all problems are solvable in half-hour sitcoms and hour-long dramas. Complex issues such as the health of our economy are covered in 90 to 120 seconds on the evening news. People running for office are expected to convey answers to pressing problems in thirty- and sixty-second advertisements. Then they are expected to keep the brief promises made ("Read my lips: no new taxes"), despite changing conditions in the laboratory.

The real world of policy making is far too complex to be captured by "time bites." Consider our economy. The American economy is no longer independent of the global economy. Our international trade today accounts for more than twice the gross national product (GNP) that it did in 1964. In addition, U.S. multinational corporations are heavily invested in the economies of other countries, and we have become increasingly dependent on jobs at home created by foreign multinationals. If we choose to reduce the value of the dollar, it will help sell our goods overseas, but it will hurt European and Asian trade, and stagnation of their economies will hurt our international trade. Raising interest rates will increase the attractiveness of the dollar, but it will hurt our own businesses. Reciprocating against European and Asian trade barriers may create a more balanced "playing field," but by now these economies have become so interdependent with ours that

Asian and European responses to unilateral U.S. actions could plunge all parties into a global recession. In the interim, while U.S. trade barriers protect some of our industries and save some jobs, they are costly for U.S. consumers. We can reduce taxes and provide tax incentives for U.S. companies to invest in equipment and research, but further tax reductions will cripple our ability to upgrade vital national infrastructure needed to compete with the economies of other nations. We could continue spending while reducing taxes, but increasing deficits will stop the government from responding to vital social and economic needs. Or we can increase taxes to fund educational, telecommunication, and transportation needs, but increasing taxes may plunge us into recession.

Given the complexity of these issues, is there a politician or a citizen who can create a meaningful 30-second answer to our economic problems? Is it likely that we can develop an answer that will work quickly and effectively and have an immediate positive impact on most Americans? What about the dozens of other complex public policy problems? Optimists believe that these problems are solvable, but it is myopic to believe that they can be solved quickly and without making mistakes. To solve them requires quality scientists in the laboratory, patience, and an electorate that has an understanding of and empathy toward the process and its complexity.

Complexity is not foreign to us. If we have trouble figuring out how to program our vcrs, then we should be able to understand how complex our societal problems are and how difficult it is to address them. Transferring such understanding to the political process, however, does not occur automatically and requires a substantial degree of empathy from citizens.

The effects of greater complexity, closer but distorted views of government and politics, and declining partisanship and lessening involvement with mediating institutions combine to create unusual pressures on our experimental form of democratic governance. It is a time when empathy and understanding stand out as critical elements in the civic culture.

SEARCHING FOR EMPATHY

The chapters that follow provide a glimpse into the political laboratory and into the lives of the men and women who don the lab coats and struggle with the experiments. Many of them are creative people who possess intelligence, dedication, and an ethic of hard work and personal commitment to doing the best they can for their community and their nation. Most of them make enormous personal and professional sacrifices to be in public office, and in this sense they are true patriots.

There are also those who don't belong in government. A few are crooked; a few are lazy. A substantial number of them carry into the laboratory ideas that seem popular but will not work. Some run for office solely for power and glory but stop working hard when they discover that they get little power and even less glory to compensate them for the hard work required to do a good job. Running for and holding office, however, expose individuals to such extensive scrutiny that the worst of the lot are weeded out. The political process probably produces many fewer liars, crooks, and cheats than are encountered outside of political life.

Nothing that is written here should be misconstrued as an apology for incompetence, misguided public policies, or those who stand in opposition to needed political reforms. Structural reforms are needed. Misguided policies need to be rectified. Officials who abuse the public trust should be ousted from office. My intention instead is to create a greater sense of understanding and empathy toward those who work in government. Strengthening understanding and empathy will not resolve our social and economic problems, but with these qualities voters can develop better judgments about what is going on in the political laboratory. In turn, the process of experimentation can continue and may yield policies that can address our present difficulties. There are alternatives to this path, but no others are compatible with how we would like to govern ourselves.

Neither am I blaming our problems on the public. Understanding and empathy are missing, but not because citizens are to blame. Their access to political knowledge is missing as well. Empathy is not created out of a vacuum and it will certainly not emerge out of the great proliferation of new information technologies. Seldom can citizens access the daily working lives of political figures and the political process in sufficient detail to develop the type of empathy needed in our democracy today. Ironically, citizens are exposed mostly to a politician's personal life when confronted with stories focusing on negatives. Many of us still remember Jimmy Carter's battle with an attack rabbit and Gerald Ford's stumbling out of airplanes. Few of us will soon forget Bill Clinton's relationship with Monica Lewinsky. These stories have saturated our airwaves but not at the request of ordinary voters.

Once citizens come to have little trust in politicians and government, politicians themselves contribute to the problem and help to create a vicious cycle that is difficult to stop. Challengers, sensing the public mood, run for office with a vengeance against incumbents and against the institutions in which they hope to serve. Even incumbents run for reelection against their own Congress, state legislature, or city council (one veteran member of Congress, for example, used the following tag line for his reelection: "Sick and tired of the mess in Washington and doing something about it").[5] Negative campaigning—taken to new levels with improved campaign technologies and armies of consultants—further reinforces negative feelings about politics. Imagine how air travel would be affected if our television channels were saturated with commercials by competing airlines showing plane crashes and blood-stained debris in vivid color while representatives from individual companies hurled accusations at one another about safety defects and improper maintenance. Yet that is precisely the type of image the public is receiving from politicians during election season. And, nowadays, election season is an ongoing occurrence.

With greater understanding and empathy we stand a chance to do what citizens are meant to do in a democracy: judge which scientists can do a better job in the laboratory. We can even deliver a message to those in the political laboratory, telling them that as long as they are working there, we want them to produce results rather than to spend their time figuring out how their own attacks on the laboratory will let them keep their jobs.

A greater sense of understanding and empathy will allow for the recruitment and retention of better-quality people to represent us. Today, the best and the brightest are not likely to make the sacrifices necessary to run for office when they know that as soon as they cross the threshold into politics they are immediately branded as unsavory characters or worse. Consider the effects on people thinking about running for office when they observe patterns of abuse aimed at officeholders such as the following. During one three-month period, the host of a local radio program directed these comments against city council members:

- One council member was accused of being a longtime pot smoker.
- One council member was labeled a "punk" and accused of being a philanderer who (the audience was told) was spotted necking with a blond reporter.
- One council member was described as whiny and brain-dead.
- One council member was described as stupid and incoherent.
- One council member was characterized as too lazy and too obsessed with food and drink (he is overweight) to pay attention to the real problems of the city.
- Two council members were accused of concocting schemes, at tax-payer expense, to defraud the IRS through phony tax deductions.
- Three of them were described as "fools and idiots."
- One was attacked as a "total, complete coward" and was referred to as "this political clown."
- All of them were attacked as being "socialists," "leftists," and "imbeciles."

None of these charges was documented, nor did the talk show host claim to have evidence for his assertions. The council members targeted by these attacks govern a city that was cited nationally as the third best run in the nation. Yet in a community of over 700,000 people, only one person called in, objecting to the remark about pot smoking. Had such a diatribe been directed at police officers, garbage collectors, or teachers, the airwaves would have been flooded with angry callers, and the show's host would have been yanked off the air. None of the newspapers in the community editorialized about this type of treatment of public officials even though it is a normal occurrence on this particular program.

Such personal attacks have become a national phenomenon. On one particular day, one national talk show focused attention on the White House family. The discussion centered on the First Lady's new haircut, which, according to host and callers alike, made her look more "butch" and reflected her political and personal orientation. This point was shortly followed by another concerning the president's "pointy" head, and how it "obviously" required extensive hair-cutting expertise.

It is hard to believe that qualified and caring citizens, interested in the welfare of their community, could listen to such invectives occurring without any accompanying public objection and still convince themselves to run for office and become the new targets of venom, hatred, and scorn. Too many of the good ones are already leaving. Twelve of the mayors I admire for their high quality of work in office have quit within the last five years despite their political popularity with the public. More than 150 members of Congress have left their posts over the last ten years as well, many of them retiring in frustration over the negativity in which officeholders operate. Tim Wirth of Colorado, who quit in disgust after only one term in the U.S. Senate, recounted how work in the laboratory changes in this climate:

> Wren and I drove across the Potomac to McLean, Va., for a supper and strategy session at the home of Chuck Robb, the Virginia Senator. . . . Chuck and his wife . . . had invited each of the 16 Democrats. . . . Everyone was tired and so was the talk. I don't recall any mention of the global environmental crisis or America's wasteful energy appetites, and only glancing references to health costs, education and defense industry conversions. Questions and comments were few and dispirited, most concerned with ways of using careful polling, target groups and ways to get reelected. I wondered what had happened to our zeal. How could we be wasting our time like this when there was so much to do. . . . Angry and frustrated, we drove home.[6]

If we want to develop better public policies to address the critical problems we face as a nation, we will need to retain people who are committed to working hard in the laboratory. We will need as well high-quality challengers who are willing to go into the laboratory to replace those who are unacceptable. We will need challengers, incumbents, and citizen activists who are committed to developing the types of structural reforms that will allow the laboratory to work better. Yet none of these changes is likely to happen unless we can develop the understanding and empathy necessary for allowing the experiment to continue.

A FOCUS ON THE LOCAL LEVEL

The chapters that follow report on what citizens seldom see. It is a story of who is working in the laboratory and the conditions under which the experiments unfold. The focus is on local officials, although often in comparison to people and institutions at the national level.

Why focus on local government? There are two major reasons. First, local governance is the area of democracy closest to the public, and it offers the greatest possibilities for developing empathy toward political figures and the democratic process. Second, local government is critical for all levels of government because it is the primary laboratory of experimentation (it has even been argued that "since the end of World War II every major domestic policy innovation in the United States has involved state and local governments").[7]

Mayors, council members, county supervisors, and state legislators do not operate in the sexiest arenas of politics. They are, however, closest to the public, their activities are more immediate and visible to citizens, and the impacts of their decisions are the most obvious and most directly felt by the public. They are also the people who work and live among us. They are our neighbors; their children go to our schools; their families picnic in our parks. If we cannot develop understanding and empathy at this level, we are not likely to do much better at the national level.

Recently, local governments have been thrust into the center of political experimentation. Until 1981, most municipalities were charged with delivering important, albeit relatively noncontroversial, "basic" services. Since 1981, with the introduction of the Reagan administration's new federalism, cities have become the new cauldrons of public policy experiments in fields relatively new to most of them. Cities now deal with public housing, environmental degradation, drug and crime problems, social services, economic development, international commerce, civil rights legislation, and political reforms. Many cities even pursue international affairs.

Corresponding to the new workload of local governments, traditional positive public evaluations of city governments have begun to decline, sometimes in seeming contradiction to good performance. The loss of faith in political institutions is spreading outside of Washington: In one recent survey of public opinion, only 9 percent of citizens indicated a great deal of confidence in state and local government, a number far below their perceptions of either Democrats or Republicans in Congress. Increasingly now at the local level, citizens are claiming lack of access and lack of trust toward officials despite the visibility and accessibility of local governments.

As we start the twenty-first century, the political life of cities is likely to increase in salience and complexity for both citizens and local elected

officials. In fact, this trend toward decentralization is spreading beyond America's borders to most democracies. The local political laboratory should become more important than at any other time in recent
memory.

The local level is also important because this political setting can
become a model for other tiers of governance. Most local governments
balance their budgets. Local officials know that their decisions will be
felt immediately by their constituents and that they must justify their
actions daily to their community's citizens. And it is at the local level
where we can still find politicians who are doing their jobs without
benefit of extravagant perks and lush salaries and who are committed to
the ideal of public service. If empathy and respect cannot increase at this
level of the political system, it is not likely that we will learn to empathize with those who work in the laboratories of the nation's capital.

3

My People

We need to create an atmosphere of respect and trust.
—President Bill Clinton at a press conference, June 17, 1993

We are having dinner with my wife's out-of-town client. She introduces us. He: "And what do you do?" Me: "I'm the mayor of this city." He: "Ah, a politician; a member of the 'liars, crooks, and cheats' club!"

In today's electronic era, we are closer visually to public officials than at any other time in our history. Through television, Bill and Hillary Clinton, Ronald Reagan, George Bush, Ted Kennedy, Newt Gingrich, and Bob Dole have been in the bedrooms and living rooms of most Americans. Governors and mayors of major cities appear almost as regularly on the local news as the television news anchors. No wonder, then, that we think we know them well. Repeatedly, I would encounter people in my city I had never met before who showed hurt and surprise in realizing that I didn't know them. They knew me—they saw me almost nightly on television. Through television, I spent many evenings with them in their homes. Why didn't I know their names and remember their faces?

The public recognizes elected officials, but it is recognition unconnected to what officials do. Many of my constituents would confuse me with their member of Congress or the television weather reporter. A number of students I taught at the University of Arizona, people who could place me in the context of "professor," would ask me if I had a brother who was the mayor they watched on television news.

I have conducted my own, unscientific poll. Once I asked a hundred people who told me that they saw me on the news (and said something positive about my "performance") what I had said or done on that particular occasion. In the overwhelming number of instances, people could not remember the verbal content of the segment. They could, however, vividly recall what I was wearing, and whether my hair was neatly combed. They would comment as well on how different I looked in person (younger, older, fatter, slimmer, more or less handsome). By the time I left office, I was voted by citizen surveys of two different newspapers as the best elected official in the region. My efforts to get on the news and to communicate with the public about the priorities of our city had led to broad public recognition of me but not necessarily to a recognition of the policies I was advocating or what I was doing with our city and their lives.

Television conveys *images* about personalities and people. It cannot, however, in sixty- or ninety-second bursts, convey much of a sense about issues or the processes of politics and governance. Yet, because citizens *see* officials today more than ever before, the viewing creates a false sense of understanding about the people who run our political affairs. Sixty seconds of access through the news constitutes substantial airtime only if you are a news producer—but how much of reality can be conveyed in sixty seconds?

Public opinion surveys typically show that while large majorities of the public disapprove of the way Congress is handling its job, the rating for their own member of Congress averages much higher approval levels. This pattern is not as contradictory as it seems. Our member of Congress has been in our bedrooms and living rooms; he or she is a personality with a warm and caring image, visually separate from the larger political context. No wonder people like their representative but vote for term limits, distrust the Congress as a whole, and profess to despise politicians.

Yet television creates a fragile image. When stories appear in the media about possible corruption and scandal, or when negative campaigning hits the airwaves and the mailboxes, the image can fracture easily. Ask George Bush how he plummeted from being the most popular president in modern times to "dead duck" in a few months without any visible change in his style or his political behavior.

It is difficult to remember how much we have changed over the last few decades with respect to our attitudes toward politics and government. Recently, a retrospective on Bobby Kennedy appeared in *Newsweek* on the anniversary of his assassination. The commentary was predictable: a complex man who was martyred, a person with flashes of greatness mixed with many shortcomings. The article reviewed what today we would call Bobby's flip-flopping on Communist witch-hunts, segregationists, and the war in Vietnam. In today's lexicon, he would be branded a ruthless professional politician, willing to do *anything* to get elected.

Three pictures accompanied the narrative. Shot in black and white, they remind us of a less glossy era, and perhaps of a time we have forgotten. In the first picture, photographed campaigning in a small Iowa town, Kennedy is standing inside an open convertible, surrounded by a pressing wall of townspeople. He is leaning over, trying to touch the dozens of outstretched hands of people desperate to make contact with him. The second picture is a cropped version of the first, set somewhere in Indiana. Kennedy's profile is framed by the smiling faces of people behind him. In the foreground, hands are reaching out, eager to touch him. In the third picture, Bobby is walking the streets of Harlem (with no visible security), surrounded by children, all clearly excited by the experience.

It is difficult to believe that these photographs were taken during horrible times. A war was raging in Asia, and soldiers were coming home mangled or dead. Citizens rioted in our central cities and faced the fire of National Guard troops. Protests and riots were exploding on college campuses. Segregationists clashed with integrationists in both the North and the South. A cultural rebellion between the generations was in full bloom. Yet even during a time of such great anger, these pictures convey a sense of trust, caring, understanding, and perhaps empathy toward a politician who suffered greatly and would soon be martyred. What elected official or candidate for office over the last two decades could evoke the feeling represented by these pictures?

Our image of politicians today is clearly a negative one. We think of them as people who are out to get something for themselves from the system: fame, glory, power, perhaps even a job. Often we see them as "professionals," a pejorative label for officeholders that connotes that politicians are willing to do anything to get reelected. Many people have come to believe that officeholders have lower ethics than the rest of society: not only willing to betray the public trust for personal gain but also having personal lives that are below the standards we feel are acceptable for those who represent us. Would you want your child to grow up to become a politician?

Yet the men and women who govern our cities are nothing like the stereotype. The people we elect in our communities look suspiciously like most other citizens. The mayor who followed me into office is a grandfather in his seventies. Before and during his terms on the city council, he owned a small painting contractor business. His wife teaches in an elementary school. He owns a modest home and drives a pickup truck. He is not a rich man. His opponents included an elementary school principal, a broadcaster, another retiree, and a manager of Tucson International Airport's janitorial division.

Tucson's recent council members have included a retiree who had served as a police officer and later worked in the mortuary business, an apartment manager, a housewife who was active in neighborhood organizations, an actress and writer, the above-mentioned manager of the airport's janitorial division, and a plumber. One-third of them are women; one-third are minorities. Few had incomes above the city's average. This council looks like its predecessors. They included a realtor, an elementary school principal, a hotel operator, a subcontractor, an accountant, a former probation officer, a newspaper reporter, a baseball coach and high school teacher, a builder with limited success, a machinist who had been in retirement for some time, a university professor, a person who owned a small accessories store, and one person who had never held a full-time job.

Our local government does not contain "professional politicians" who are moving up the career ladder. Two of the last three mayors had some previous experience in government, having served as council members. One of the council members served in the state legislature before running for city office. The rest had come from nonpolitical walks of life and will leave politics after serving on the governing body. With one exception, throughout the entire history of our state, no mayor or council member has ever gone on to higher office. None of these people fits the profile of ambitious political professional, carefully cultivating his or her future at the expense of the community.

DIVERSITY IN REPRESENTATION

The people who run my city are not that much different from those around the country. A recent mayor of Ft. Worth sold greeting cards for a living before entering government. A mayor of Seattle was a local broadcaster. My friend from the Portland, Oregon, city council, a mother with seven children, was a neighborhood activist before running for office. She served with a mayor who was a tavern owner. A pivotal member of the Charlotte, North Carolina, city council ran a small business before running for office, and after sending her children to college, she finished her term and went on to law school. Few of my acquaintances in other cities fit the stereotype of those in elected positions: Seldom did I run into a lawyer, an "experienced" political pro, or a person of substantial wealth.

Representatives at the local level are actually beginning to look like the citizens they are meant to represent, and much of this change has occurred recently. There are now over six times as many African American elected officials in city and county governments as there were in 1970. Nearly half of the top ten cities of the nation have elected African American mayors. Likewise, the overwhelming number of Hispanic elected officials are in local office, and their numbers have increased by over 60 percent in a bit over a decade. In large cities, nearly half of all council members come from minority groups.

Moreover, the vast majority of women officeholders are found in state and local governments. The numbers of councilwomen grew more than fourfold nationally in less than two decades. Women mayors are in office in about 15 percent of our cities, and this figure rises to over 20 percent in cities with populations over 100,000. Women have governed the largest cities, including Houston, San Francisco, Dallas, San Diego, San Antonio, Phoenix, Portland, Salt Lake City, and Washington, D.C. Nor are women mayors simply figureheads: More than one-quarter of the cities with mayoral veto power over legislation are governed by women.

Of course, the ranks of local officials still reflect the residues of discrimination in society. Despite the enormous gains in recent years, women, particularly, are still underrepresented in local councils, just as they are underrepresented among the ranks of the economic elite in our cities. While the glass ceiling is cracking faster in city hall than outside, it has not yet disappeared.

WHY RUN FOR OFFICE?

Why would anyone decide to run for office to win a job that pays terrible wages, requires impossibly long hours, is the focus of constant criticism and scrutiny, and offers little or no prospect for future advancement? It is very difficult to identify the real motivation of these people, and perhaps they themselves are not fully aware of all the factors that lead them to run for office. Yet a few commonalties are evident. In most cases, local officials were asked to run by either friends or fellow activists involved in one cause or another, or by their political party after they had publicly surfaced on community issues. I was approached by the county chair of my party before my first run for city office. She had already asked five other people to run against the incumbent, but all of them had turned her down. I initially rejected the offer as well, but she appealed to my sense of self-worth: "How can you criticize the incumbent without trying to do something about getting rid of him when you have the chance?" I decided to run more out of a sense of not wanting to feel like a hypocrite than for any other reason. Five of the seven people on my city council were similarly drafted. Two of them were asked to run by environmental groups, two others by neighborhood organizations, and one was pressed into politics by his political party.

June's story is typical. She is a mother of two children and an activist in her community. She worked with children's groups to promote conservation and recycling efforts, and she worked with environmentalists to protect the national forest near her city. When an opening occurred on the city council, she was asked to run by her friends. At first, she turned them down, believing that she was doing enough. Finally, she was persuaded that the opportunity to serve would increase her success in fighting for her political goals. She ran and won.

Bud may have been even more reluctant than June to run for office. Although he had worked for scores of other candidates, he was not a slick campaigner. Furthermore, managing a small business meant that campaigning would occur only at nights and on weekends, and he was not a young man. But he was loyal to his party, and his loyalty to the city was strong as well. He was persuaded to run and served in office for twenty years, long after he would have retired from his business.

On one level, many of us ran because we were asked and found it hard to say no to those who asked us. Yet the matter of motivation is far more complex than whether or not one gets drafted. Most people who run have been active in their community. Their backgrounds reflect a sense of commitment to their city: a desire to make life better and a willingness to help shape the future for their families, friends, and neighbors. Running for office takes this commitment to another level and increases the opportunity to make a difference. Few are willing to run unless they have a burning desire to do something—to implement critical projects or proposals—for their community.

On another level, being asked to run for office also touches the ego and appeals to those who have a strong sense of self-confidence. Many activists have been asked to run who ultimately declined the offer. I have approached numerous good people with the idea of convincing them to run for office. Many of them thought hard and long about the idea of exposing themselves before the public and found the idea repugnant. In this respect, people in public office are different from those who choose not to run. They are usually confident of their abilities, believe that they are good problem solvers, feel that they can hold up against the pressure and stress, and feel strongly that they have something of great value to contribute to the policy process.

One particular survey has underscored the motivational basis for seeking office. A major study looked at a broad cross section of 3,000 political leaders and activists (activists make up the larger world from which nearly all candidates are eventually recruited) and studied them for more than two decades.[8] The researchers found that, irrespective of the political party or gender, the most important dimension motivating activists was a concern for "policy issues and the state of society." The least important factor was political ambition. Although some have claimed that we have more professional politicians than ever before, the trend over the twenty years of this study revealed that political ambition is no more important a motivating force now than it was in the 1960s.

Surveys like these, however, cannot probe below the surface to reveal the more complex nature of the people who become our public officials. I found that the ones I worked with came into office possessing personal courage along with their convictions. Consider the mayor who succeeded me. A long time ago he was a teacher, but his sense of right and wrong was so strong that he gave up a promising career rather than succumb to the humiliation involved with the Communist witch-hunts of the 1950s. A liberal and a strong civil libertarian, he served during World War II in the Marine Corps and helped to desegregate our community in the 1950s by participating in the first organized sit-ins of the city's lunch counters.

Our council members were no less courageous. One earned a doctor of education degree from Emory in Atlanta when that city was still segregated and blacks were not welcome. I was with him at a conference in a southern city one evening when he was heckled in a bar by two drunk white couples. While I was nervously eyeing the exit, he rose from his barstool, winked at me, walked over to the tallest and loudest of the four, introduced himself, and started to chat. Within five minutes, his new friends were buying us drinks.

The person who took his seat at the council table was an ex-cop who saw duty in both Tucson and Chicago. Next to him sat a man whose courage had been tested in Vietnam. With him served a council member who protested the war and earned the hatred of thousands for his convictions. Sitting next to him was a woman who ran the risk of weekly abuse by critics for her public writings. The woman she replaced started her professional career as a probation officer and battled substantial gender discrimination to become a successful professional in the community. Virtually all of the businesspeople who served on the city council took great personal risks and sacrificed much to maintain and develop their businesses and then switched to other business endeavors when the marketplace was no longer favorable.

FAMILY LIVES AT RISK

These people are courageous in another sense as well: They come into office knowing the risks they are taking in their personal lives, yet they take the risks anyway. The public often thinks of elected officials as political "animals," and sees them only in the context of the offices they occupy. In reality, they fill a number of additional roles, including spouse, parent, and child.

When we see politicians in a family context, the reality of family life is seldom seen. Spouses and children appear before television cameras on the campaign trail and on election night as the returns come in. Spouses are asked to stand up and wave as they are introduced at formal functions and endless chicken dinners. There are no photographs or videotape of my wife's gentle touch on my knee before I start to speak, offering the support and affection she feels. There is no public evidence of her sitting in the third row of a hostile audience, conveying to me in the intensity of her stare that I am not alone. No public record exists of my friend Jim trying to protect his family from the abuse being heaped upon him (and indirectly on them) by a particularly nasty radio personality. The public does not see the councilwoman who wrings her hands while asking me how she should deal with a nine-year-old son who came home crying and angry because he found out that people on the radio were calling his mother a "stupid idiot" and a "crazy woman." There is no formal record of the endless conflicts between public officials and their private spouses, arguing about the lack of "quality time" for the family. Few of us think about the president worrying about his daughter's feelings when she hears her father being called "Slick Willie" and "Willie the Weenie" on national radio.

Most people who attain office come to public life as part of a family. Of the hundreds of officials with whom I have worked, I can think of only five who were not married and fewer than a dozen who did not have children. Yet the family becomes a two-edged sword in their lives. On the one hand, its importance is obvious: It is the primary place "in which people can give and receive love, compassion, nurturance, and psychic support."[9] For politicians, the family may be the only setting in which they are not judged, evaluated, or critiqued on a regular basis. It is a place to retreat, to search for comfort, and to disengage from the stresses of public life.

On the other hand, the pressures on an elected official's family are enormous. Time itself is a constant source of friction. Meetings occur at night and on weekends. Particularly for local politicians, emergencies abound and seem to come around midnight or later. I had a strict rule that two nights a week would belong to my family. I rarely remember a week when the "rule" went unbroken. Often I worked every night, seven days a week. I used to joke in public that there were times when I would come home and my faithful Airedale would growl at me because he no longer remembered my scent. Friends and citizens would always laugh, but other elected officials would respond by telling their stories of family stresses, as long as citizens were not around to hear them.

My first marriage of fifteen years dissolved under the relentless pressures imposed by public office. I worked too many hours in two different jobs. I seldom had time to be at home. When we snatched time away from work to go to dinner or to a movie, we never escaped public attention and requests for assistance from constituents. When we decided to escape public scrutiny by hiding at home, the telephone would ring constantly. Today's official is accessible. Particularly in local government, an unlisted phone number is a statement to citizens that you don't care about them. Anyone who wanted to do so could look up my home number in the directory. Many took advantage of the opportunity. When citizens were not calling, their places in our lives were quickly filled by my staff, city department heads, or other elected officials, stealing minutes from their busy schedules to catch up on business they couldn't finish during "working hours."

When I tried to involve my ex-spouse in my public activities, she became invisible. No matter how intelligent, attractive, or quick he or she is, no spouse can compete with the power of an officeholder in public. Spouses end up standing at public gatherings with frozen smiles, feigning interest in conversations repeated dozens of times, politely laughing at jokes that weren't all that funny the first time they heard them. Spouses begin to shrink in public until they disappear in the shadow of the council member, the mayor, the governor, the legislator. Yet they are not allowed to disappear. Their absence in public is a sign that "something is wrong." Even those spouses who are true partners in the political adventure (and there are many who are) are ultimately rejected by the public because they are not the ones elected. They are told in dozens of ways that they are less important than the person with whom they live. Susan, a council member in a large eastern city, a person who I thought was happily married, told me: "It is a constant friction in our marriage that my husband has come to feel that his job is just not as challenging, not as important as mine. And in our daily outings into the world, he is reminded of it at every turn."

A marriage is meant to be a partnership between equals, and this imbalance in the relationship proves difficult for many couples. Finding help when the marriage is in trouble is virtually impossible. The public glare is so strong that few politicians will seek professional assistance and run the risk of public focus and discussion over the collapsing marriage. Yet working out these problems without professional assistance is quite problematic. When coupled with the responsibilities involved in raising children, the stresses of family life can become overwhelming.

Sherry, an elected official from a city in Ohio, refers to one aspect of the family dilemma facing public figures as the "run/divorce trap. After a while, you face the prospect of running for reelection. By now, nothing would please your spouse better than your choosing not to run again. But would our marriage survive if I decided not to run because of him and blamed him for it for the rest of our lives together? Whichever decision I make is going to harm us."

For too many officials, the stresses involved in balancing family and politics lead beyond tolerable limits. Nearly two decades ago, even during a gentler era of politics, a survey of state legislators found that nearly half of those who voluntarily left office did so because their positions interfered with their families. Since then, politicians have been facing even stronger pressures, and the effects on their families are even worse today. All of the divorces on our city council occurred in the last few years. I can remember virtually no cases of divorce among our city's officials in the 1970s; many then, as well as now, avoided permanent separations but continued to lead stressful, unhappy lives.

Politicians, of course, are not all alike, and neither are their circumstances. A lucky few have marriages that have endured the stresses of public office, and there are even the very rare instances where the spouse remains an active political partner. But the preponderant trend is in the other direction.

STRUGGLING AGAINST THE GLASS CEILING

While elected officials may be quite similar when it comes to family stresses, when it comes to gender differences women in office are exposed to many more hardships and in ways that are quite different from men. Historically, women entered public office in far fewer numbers than their male counterparts and bore the extra burden of being pioneers in a male world. Traditionally, professional women have had to meet the rigors of their professions along with family responsibilities to a far greater degree than men. As a result, most of the women who used to claim their share of political power did so at an older age, after raising children.

Even without children at home, however, women in local government face additional challenges, including the problem of working in a man's world. One councilwoman in Florida—who was the only female on her council—talked honestly in private about how lonely she felt on a predominantly male governing body. She said that she felt excluded even though the men worked to integrate her into the political process. "When we took breaks during council meetings," she said, "I had this incredible urge to follow them into the bathroom. I just knew that they were having the important discussions there." Then she paused and said, "If I could have just gone in there with them, then somehow I knew I could relate better to what was going on at the meetings." Another councilwoman from the Midwest told me that when she first met with leaders of the business community they confessed to her that they "didn't know how to talk to me because I was a woman." One of them suggested that if she took up golfing, maybe they could relate to her better.

Over the past decade, larger numbers of women officials have joined the lonely pioneer woman. Yet the increasing numbers of women in local government have not necessarily meant that men now treat women as equals. One councilwoman from a southeastern city with a history of electing women to office remembered well the difficulty in overcoming gender-role stereotyping: "I thought that I was equal to the men. But John treated me like his daughter, Jim treated me like his lover, and Fred treated me like his younger sister. All three came to reject me because I wanted them to treat me as a council member, and I refused to accept their roles for me."

Even when treated as equals in the political arena, women must continue to juggle political, professional, spousal, and maternal responsibilities. The stress women face under these burdens is enormous, and more so than for men, since female officials believe to a far greater extent than men that they can be good politicians as well as good parents and spouses. And taking on the role of "superwoman" is no easy task. Jane is a local official in California, balancing her elected responsibilities with a career that she now pursues only part time while in office. She is married and has two children, ages six and thirteen. She gets up at five in the morning, prepares a lunch for both children, gets breakfast ready, and reads two newspapers while the rest of the family sleeps. On her way to the office she takes the younger one to school. Here's her view of the superwoman role:

> My thirteen-year-old thinks I'm doing something important, but my six-year-old greatly resents the little time I spend with him. When people ask him what I do, he gets surly and says, "Mom talks and goes to meetings." Recently, he has begun to act out his frustrations in school and at home. Every two months we have a family crisis from it. And I feel so guilty. I think of myself as a feminist, but many a day I think that it's primarily my responsibility to deal with the children. If only I would spend more time with them, . . . if only I could give more time to them and my spouse. . . . I just tend to feel most of the blame here.

LOW AND HIGH ESTEEM

As politicians differ according to the effects of gender-based roles, they also differ with respect to their psychological makeup. Some are psychological entrepreneurs who seek office and try to use politics to satisfy a variety of psychological needs. While the majority of politicians seek office with policy interests in mind, there are those who seek fame and success above all else in order to satisfy drives internal to their personalities. These are, of course, the people whom we fear and distrust the most. Yet I found these politicians to be in a distinct minority among the ranks of local officials across the nation.

We expect that people who run for office are likely to be somewhat different from those who choose not to run. Their circumstances often differ from typical citizens, allowing them the time and opportunity to seek office. It would not be surprising to discover that they differ from the public as well in their need for power and achievement. Indeed, researchers have shown that officeholders differ from the public on attributes related to self-esteem. Nevertheless, and especially at the local level, few politicians can serve and survive in office if they are primarily psychological entrepreneurs.

Consider Jim, a council member from a city in Illinois. In psychological terms, Jim is a politician with low self-esteem. Constantly frustrated in his professional career, he found few opportunities for advancement.

His activities in civic groups were not unique enough to propel him into a position of respect in the community. Yet, miraculously, he was asked to run for the city council. When he ran, he seldom talked about issues. His themes focused on trust, respect, and competence. With little opposition, he won.

Why did Jim run for office? Politicians with low self-esteem use public office to seek position and acceptance. They are not the candidates who will run aggressive campaigns; we will find them when public scrutiny is at its lowest and conflicts in elections are at a minimum. They are not likely to take great risks in public, and they are also not likely to challenge incumbents, and since elections without incumbents and without conflicts are relatively rare, the number of politicians with low self-esteem who hold office is low as well.

What will low-esteem politicians do in office? The answer is not much. Jim worked few hours, avoided conflict when possible, and enjoyed little success in helping to forge public policies. Policy making involves conflict, compromise, and bargaining. Because he avoided conflict, his effectiveness on the council was virtually nonexistent. He could have become more effective by using the media to reach the public about pressing issues, but he was ill at ease in front of cameras. At the same time, he complained incessantly to colleagues and staff that he was being ignored. Finally, he left office for a job in the private sector. He was frustrated there as well. Hoping to recover his prestige and status, he returned as a candidate once more, but this time he found himself in a high-conflict campaign, did badly, and was decisively defeated. He fit the classic low-esteem mold: "He sees politics as a refuge. . . . Low esteem politicians want responsibility and recognition without the demands and responsibilities that go with them. But that is a virtually unattainable situation."[10]

Jim's tenure in public office was brief. Some low-esteem politicians can stay in office for longer periods, but only during times when the political system is enjoying the public's confidence. During more turbulent times, their low self-esteem will speed their exit from government.

The public may be even more fearful of another type of psychological entrepreneur: high-esteem politicians who are "attracted to power, find its exercise appealing, admire those who use it," and "seek and thrive on visibility . . . because public attention is one of their major incentives for pursuing a political career."[11] For them, as for those with low self-esteem, the primary motive in running for office is the pursuit of personal psychological gain separate from broad policy interests.

Joan was one such candidate from a northeastern city. When an incumbent in her district looked weak, she jumped at the chance to run. She said later: "This was my time. I ran out of challenges in my business, and now it was my chance to shine in public." She was gregarious and outgoing, moving rapidly from one campaign event to another, happily plunging into crowds and shaking hands. Her speeches were peppered with jokes, and she stole liberally from the issue positions of fellow candidates.

Once in office, she worked hard at her job. She loved the contact with constituents, politicians, and the press. She plunged into virtually any issue or conflict with relish and abandon, but many of her answers were off-the-cuff and unworkable. She spent much time cutting ribbons, giving speeches, and making herself readily available for the cameras and the reporters. While the low-esteem politician is usually unavailable for comment, she was practically unavoidable for comment when the media lurked nearby.

There are personality aspects of high-esteem politicians that are important to the job of an elected official: Using power and communicating with the public through the media are essential for developing public policies. However, politicians who are driven by a lust for power and recognition often come to office with an empty slate. Their lack of policy direction and clear priorities will lead to their downfall. They fight for the enjoyment of being in battle and for the right to fight other battles later on. As a result, they stumble into positions that are indefensible and take on too many issues. Soon they grow stale in the eyes of the public and lose credibility with their colleagues.

By the end of her first year in office, her colleagues considered Joan an embarrassment to them. The reporters grew tired of her jokes and the difficulty of reporting on actions that were too unpredictable and confusing. Citizens at council meetings and at town halls began to complain that she was superficial and "flippant" about their concerns, although her staff worked hard to respond to constituent problems. Her lack of direction meant, according to her own aide, that "she was into everything and prioritized nothing." She and her staff ended up working horribly long hours but, overwhelmed, were getting nowhere. The long hours finally affected all other aspects of her life, including her personal relationships and her business. Finally, she gave up and quit politics.

Having high self-esteem is not enough to be successful in office. While a good sense of self and psychic gratification from being in the limelight may be enough to motivate people to run for office, these attributes are not enough to sustain elected officials once they are in office. Without a clear sense of policy direction, high-esteem individuals will fail as surely as those with low esteem. There is simply too much to do and too many issues from which to choose. Without clear policy direction, high-esteem politicians will be overwhelmed by the day-to-day work or flounder hopelessly on political seas until they come to be rejected by both their colleagues and the voters.

Psychological entrepreneurs are exposed in local politics because the individual scrutiny of elected officials is greater at the local level than at other levels of government. Media scrutiny is made easier because local governing bodies are small, and both low- and high-esteem politicians become too visible to the public. This is not necessarily the case for psychological entrepreneurs who manage to get to Congress. In a legislative body of 435 members, or even one with 100 senators, psychological entrepreneurs can thrive without encountering the scrutiny to which local officials are subjected.

SEARCHING FOR CORRUPTION

Most people found in local office resemble those citizens in our community whom we respect and would like to have representing us: They are hard workers and, usually, intelligent people. They come to politics with a rich family life. They bring with them a strong sense of civic responsibility and a sense of caring about their community. The pure power seekers and the ones with low self-esteem usually do not make it into office or are soon washed out.

Yet the cycle of mistrust about government and politics has become so strong that when decent people travel down the political road, they are instantly judged in ways very different from the ways we judge people outside of the political process. In a bitter retrospective on his term on the city council, one former official told me: "I lived in this community for twenty years, and everyone I came into contact with trusted and liked me. As soon as I got on the city council, it meant an instant loss of credibility. All of a sudden, anyone who didn't like what I was doing would immediately challenge my integrity and motives."

Elected officials today know that serving in office means that they risk ruining their reputations because the climate of distrust accentuates scandal at all levels of government. Corrupt and self-serving politicians deserve their ruin if they betray the public trust. Unfortunately, the vast majority of elected officials, although they have done nothing illegal or immoral, are burned as well by the flames of scandal when opponents and the media search for wrongdoing that may not be there.

The moment one enters into the political arena and becomes a "public figure," the rules of judgment change. If I want to smear your reputation, you have recourse to slander and libel laws through the courts. Those same laws do not protect public figures. The legal principle of "innocent until proven guilty" is not available for politicians. And when large numbers of people begin to distrust government and the officials they put into office, the political process can shift easily from debate about policy to attacks on character and integrity. In fact, it is much easier to attack the integrity of politicians than to engage in serious debate about complex issues. It is far easier to rally opposition to "crooks" than to oppose on policy grounds those who seek to change the status quo.

Consider the following events: Years ago, a new group of people was elected to our city council. They wanted to allocate a greater share of tax dollars for social service programs, public transportation, and historic preservation. The mayor was philosophically opposed to these changes, and suddenly his friend the police chief started to play an ever larger role in the budget process by publicly speaking out and arguing that the city council's misplaced priorities meant that the police were understaffed and the city was in danger. The council members brought the chief before the council and asked him to explain his statements. He told them that the "trouble" in the city's parks could not be contained as long as he had insufficient resources to deal with troublemakers. The council members responded by directing the chief to reprioritize his officers to address the problem. The council members met again with the chief a few weeks before his new budget was due for discussion and asked about the "trouble" in the parks. He indicated that the situation was now under control. Then, a couple of days before the budget hearings, he informed reporters that the parks were so dangerous that he would not allow his own family to use them.

At this point the council members decided to meet in executive session to deal with the chief's blatant manipulation of the budget process. The mayor decided not to come to the executive session. In the privacy of an executive session reserved for personnel matters, council members angrily vented their feelings about the chief. At times, believing that their words could never become public (it is illegal to release transcripts of executive sessions), they allowed their anger to erupt into the type of vulgar language they would never use in public. The meeting concluded with no action taken.

The mayor struck back the next day. Here was a golden opportunity to change the terms of the debate. Instead of arguing about appropriate police staffing versus the need for social programs, the mayor raised the specter of scandal and corruption. He had copies made of the transcript of the session, held a press conference, released the transcript, and denounced the council for holding an "illegal" executive session. Then he demanded a public outcry and legal sanctions.

The press had a field day. The newspapers carried the events as if the council had stolen from public coffers. One television station aired a special "reenactment" with reporters standing in for council members and reading to the cameras the lines spoken at the executive session, particularly emphasizing the "expletives" used by council members. The newspapers expanded their coverage as well by printing the transcript verbatim. One newspaper ran editorials vilifying the council, defending the chief, and praising the mayor.

Then the other shoe fell. The county attorney, keenly aware of the increasing culture of mistrust toward politicians, indicted the entire council on felony charges for violating the state's open-meetings laws. The potential punishment: felony conviction, jail time, and eviction from office. For months, individual council members went through hell trying to defend themselves against the charges. Along with their official, family, and private work responsibilities, they spent their waking hours meeting with lawyers and preparing for court. During the trial, the prosecutors attacked them as if they were veteran criminals. When the trial ended, the superior court judge found all officials innocent and admonished the prosecution for going through with "this legal spectacle."

Never before or since these events had this particular city council been exposed to the amount of news coverage evoked by the executive session "scandal." No issue, no election, no problem, no public policy can match the drama and excitement that accompany accusations of wrongdoing even when the accusations are incorrect. Years afterward, journalists and political opponents still searched for new cases of open-meetings violations (and sometimes publicly accused officeholders) in hopes of finding another juicy scandal.

For the mayor, it was much easier to go the route of accusing the council of wrongdoing than to engage in debate about budget priorities or about the appropriateness of the police chief's behavior. Even so, scandalmongering would have been a useless exercise unless the public was willing to believe, the press anxious to expose, and the county attorney eager to upgrade his reputation by lodging charges, whether or not they could be upheld in court. By the end of this sorry mess, the newspapers had sold a few extra papers, television news programs had temporarily increased the size of their audiences, and the mayor and the county attorney had briefly appeared as public crusaders. The big losers were the officeholders who were willing to take on an entrenched police chief and his budgetary priorities. Despite their victory in court, some left office for good, while some of the others never took major risks again.

The public lost as well. The real debate about policy priorities never received the public attention it deserved. Meanwhile, large sums of public and private dollars were spent frivolously on a court case while serious cases were jamming the court docket. Finally, good citizens came to feel less good about their government and about a city council that had done nothing wrong.

This was not an isolated incident, and it did not happen in only one city. Other such spectacles occur throughout our cities and in Washington on a regular basis. Congressman Newt Gingrich became a leader of the Republican opposition and eventually Speaker of the U.S. House of Representatives because he shifted the terms of the debate from arguing about Democratic policy initiatives to accusing Democrats of personal wrongdoing and corrupt practices. Nearby, charges of scandal and personal irresponsibility routinely washed over the Clinton White House and particularly escalated as the president's popularity began to increase. When one year the charges hit around Christmas, they brought an angry retort from the First Lady: "It hurts. Even though you're a public figure, which means apparently in America anybody can say anything about you. Even public figures have feelings and families and reputations."[12]

The scandal process works for those who wield the sword of scandal: The integrity of the accused is severely impaired, irrespective of guilt or innocence. Meanwhile, the innocent are harmed along with the guilty, and the higher up one goes in the political system, the larger the cost for politicians. One study of recent scandals reviewed a case in Washington of a member of the Justice Department who spent five years being investigated and incurred legal fees in excess of $1 million before he was exonerated.[13] Another person who was also found not guilty after a long ordeal asked for reimbursement of the million dollars he had spent defending himself. The court denied his request, arguing that he was treated just like any other citizen.

Once cynicism, distrust, and a lack of empathy dominate the civic culture, scandal and character assassination begin to replace the debate over public policies at all levels of government. Had teachers, office workers, police officers, or mechanics faced such inquisition and had they been forced to pay hundreds of thousands of dollars to defend themselves when they had done nothing wrong, there would have been an enormous public outcry. When the targets are politicians, there is only a diminution of trust and confidence in those who govern. Meanwhile, the effect on the civic culture is incalculable as the stench of scandal further reinforces negative attitudes about the political process.

The impact on the political laboratory is equally negative. Experiments cannot be run successfully when the emphasis is placed not on the effects of the experiment but on charges of scandal relating to the behavior of the experimenters, in and out of the political laboratory. When too much time is spent on the characteristics of the laboratory personnel and insufficient evaluation occurs of the experiment itself, then the people in the lab coats will spend more and more of their time focusing on their public image at the expense of conducting successful experiments. It is also unlikely that good people will continue to try to find a place in the laboratory if they have to entertain such personal costs for themselves and their families.

Citizens want their elected officials to work hard, to choose public service over personal glory and political advancement, and to be in touch with the needs of their constituents. These are by and large the types of people who serve the public at the local level. Yet the absence of empathy and a loss of civic culture are spawning a pattern of mistrust toward the very people who are striving to do their best to represent us. It is too much to expect that those who wish to stop the policy direction of government will curb their diatribes against those who hold the reigns of power. Nor is it likely that the media will cease to exploit potential scandals or caricatures of politicians unless citizens begin to say that they are more interested in policy outcomes than in the skewering of their elected officials. When citizens begin to complain that they would rather hear about what is happening to their president's health-care reform than about charges that he may have disrobed before someone in Arkansas many years ago, then both political opponents and the media will reevaluate their tactics. Such an enlightened citizenry, however, is not likely to emerge without the development of greater empathy toward what actually happens in the political laboratory.

4

The Perks of Office

"I've run for office and I've discovered that the people in government never work from conviction."[14]

"The Senator from Kentucky holds up a huge mock-up of a stamp on the floor of the Senate in the middle of the campaign finance reform debate and says: 'That's what this is all about . . . food stamps for us!' "[15]

Two major indictments of politics and politicians revolve around the issue of "perks." Many Americans believe that billions of tax dollars are wasted on expensive or useless programs, in part by lining the pockets of political officials—if not directly through bribes and graft, then at least by providing valuable and expensive "perks" for officeholders. Using the laboratory analogy, the perks taken by the people in the lab coats, if true, diminish the resources needed to carry out successful experiments for pressing problems.

Another belief held by many citizens is that public officials are "out of touch" with the public and that part of the insulation of representatives from their constituents stems from the broad range of "perks" cushioning the bumps and bruises of ordinary life for politicians. According to this belief, experimenters in the political laboratory misjudge unsuccessful experiments as being successful because they are too insulated to understand the effects of their experiments. In either case, the issue of perks for politicians has become a symbol of what is wrong with politics and government.

Understandably, the blood boils as the lists of special privileges are made public: free check-cashing and check-bouncing privileges for members of Congress; limousine service for the leadership on Capitol Hill and for White House staff; $200 haircuts on the Tarmac at LAX for the president; free vacations and bogus fact-finding missions to exotic places; luxurious exercise rooms in Congress. The list seems endless.

Witness one newspaper's coverage of the abuses perpetrated by a former chair (Dan Rostenkowski) of the Ways and Means Committee of the U.S. House of Representatives. The thrust of the story was that even if the specific case was extreme, it typified an attitude generally shared by officeholders, who were said to be "bumming off fat cats or dipping into campaign funds . . . that guarantee Mr. Rostenkowski and many of his colleagues a life of blissful bondage."[16] Rostenkowski's transgressions went beyond perks, including using honoraria he was not allowed to keep, coordinating speaking engagements with vacation times to avoid violating congressional gifts and travel rules, and stealing from his office's stamp fund. Rostenkowski's story (for which he ultimately went to jail and lost his seat in the U.S. Congress) is underscored by numerous other exposés. For example, the media also profiled the perks of office for both the majority leader and the minority leader in the U.S. House of Representatives. These perks included beach cottage rentals, limousines, expensive restaurant tabs, luxury box seats at sporting events, ski lodge vacations, and free air transportation. It is easy for the public to conclude from stories like these that political life is feathered by a continuous flow of perks not just for people in Washington but for those at all levels of government.

For the vast majority of local elected officials, this list of perks is as alien as for most citizens outside of politics. Mayors and council members receive few tangible rewards for their efforts. The most significant reward is the salary they receive, which in many cities is set either by the city's charter or by the state legislature. As a result, most local officials are grossly underpaid compared to both their federal and their private-sector counterparts.

Consider the salaries of council members and mayors in the fifty largest cities of America. Some of these mayors receive salaries as low as $2,000 annually; some council members do not have salaries beyond

$1,200 annually. Even the best-paid mayor in the United States—the mayor of New York City, responsible for a budget that runs in the billions and charged with the welfare of over 9 million people—gets a salary no higher than a member of Congress, who represents fewer than 450,000 people. Of course, the typical salary of mayors is a great deal less than found in New York City; it averages about $62,000 annually when the five largest cities in America are removed from the equation.

The compensation story gets worse when we consider city council members. Nationally, the average salary of these officials in the top fifty cities is under $30,000, and once the five largest cities are excluded, salaries go down to $25,000. Forty percent of the fifty largest cities provide salaries for council members at such low levels that the compensation for these officials places them below the real poverty line for a family of four. Seven of the mayors in the top fifty cities also receive annual salaries that place them below the real poverty line.

Are these people compensated better than people outside government? Taking into account the hours they work, the pressures they encounter, and the responsibilities they have, they are grossly underpaid for their work, regardless of the standard of comparison. Perhaps comparisons to sports figures or television personalities are inappropriate, but as an example, Shaquille O'Neal, at twenty-one, made $3 million annually to play basketball, and Connie Chung earned over $2 million annually as co-anchor of *CBS News*. Comparisons, however, with people in a broad variety of fields still reveal how little compensation local officials receive. A comparison with the wages earned by typical Americans provides some interesting yardsticks:

- In twenty of the nation's fifty largest cities, council members receive salaries lower than the median wage for the nation's workers. In fact, the average annual salary of all council members in forty-six of the nation's largest cities is barely above the median wage.
- The nation's high school principals are paid more than twice the average of council members' salaries, and their wages match the average annual salary of mayors in the nation's top fifty cities.
- Telephone repair technicians in Reno, Nevada, are paid twice the average salary of council members in the nation's top fifty cities.
- Hotel desk clerks in Las Vegas earn more than the salary paid the mayor of Dallas, Ft. Worth, Miami, Oklahoma City, Sacramento, or San Antonio.

Comparing the salaries of public officials with private-sector salaries on the basis of financial responsibility shows an even bleaker picture. The mayors of the fifty largest cities in the United States are responsible for budgets that range from $250 million to $3 billion. Compared to them, the CEOs of relatively small corporations (those with average sales below $100 million) earn base salaries and benefits many times more than the compensation of mayors.[17] The contrast in compensation between council members and professional classes in the general workforce shows an even greater pattern of differences. Virtually no professional classification is paid a salary as low as council members, with the possible exception of social workers. Even public school teachers, who are chronically undervalued and are often at the mercy of bond elections and tax overrides influencing their salaries, receive compensation in excess of the salaries of local elected officials.

Are these comparisons unfair? One argument against better council and mayoral salaries has been that often these officeholders don't work full-time. Yet in the country's fifty top cities (the sites for these comparisons), it is impossible to do a decent job either on the city council or as mayor without putting in an amount of time well in excess of what we consider to be a full-time job requiring full-time compensation.

Most local officials will grumble in private about their salaries, but they know when they run for office that they will not be fairly compensated. Many local officials know that they must hold a second job and accept the fact that they will still lose income to serve in office. In my case, the combined income I received from public office and my reduced compensation from my professional job still cost me between 10 percent and 20 percent of my income annually during a decade and a half of public service.

Unlike members of Congress, local officials are not paid honoraria for their numerous speaking engagements even if they are asked to speak and consult outside of their jurisdictions during their terms of office. As an elected official I gave nearly 500 speeches to audiences in my city and around the nation. I was offered an honorarium on only three occasions, and I refused each time. Conversations with other local officials have underscored the fact that this practice is typical for them as well.

Apart from salaries, other types of tangible benefits are provided to elected officials in many cities. These often vary with levels of salary.

For example, automatic expense accounts for officials are typical only where salaries are extremely low. Where salaries are higher for both mayor and council members, there is no automatic annual expense account.

Office expenses for elected officials in most cities are typically set through individual mayoral or council member budgets and become part of the public budgeting process by being voted upon in public meetings by the city council. These budgets are carefully scrutinized by the media as elected officials compete with one another and their pre-decessors to keep costs as low as possible. Few politicians would want to publicly increase their office expenses while denying support to vital departments or to vital social and economic programs, or to run the risk of being perceived as raising fees or taxes to feather their own nests. Council member Dennis, from a large northwestern city, was so con-cerned about this issue that he took only one public trip outside of his community during a twelve-year career. He was able to show virtually no office travel costs, but he never had the opportunity to see what other cities were doing, and he failed to learn from their experiences. The benefit he gained was one story a year in the local newspaper showing that he spent less than his colleagues.

The public and the media may view vehicle expenses and travel reimbursements as perks even though they constitute fair compensation for conducting public business. Most council members—when not in their offices—are driving to meetings, traveling to rezoning sites, or going to various emergencies around town. I found myself averaging over 20,000 miles per year driving to various official activities within the city's limits. In fact, the car became a second office when the days were exceedingly long. I would grab a stack of phone messages while leaving my office and return phone calls while driving. The advent of cellular phones has become the ultimate gift (and curse) for overbur-dened officeholders.

What other perks are granted to local officials? Not many. Here is a list of perks available to elected officials in my city: free parking at city hall; free parking at the airport when flying on official business; free popcorn at council meetings; free sandwiches if council meetings last through the evening; free police surveillance when physically threat-ened; advance purchase of tickets to concerts at the municipal conven-tion center.

I didn't realize the difference between the perception and reality of perks until I started visiting local elementary schools during our city's annual "love of reading" program. After reading to a class, we would have time for questions. Within the first five minutes, the questions would come regarding the trappings of office, straight from the mouths of ten-year-olds: "Where is your limousine?" "Where is your chauffeur?" "Where are your bodyguards?" The disappointment on the faces of these children when hearing that I had none of the accoutrements of office spoke clearly of the vision of politicians communicated to them by their parents and the media.

Local officials do more than go to meetings and give speeches. Many of them are active in regional, state, national, and international activities on behalf of their cities. Other efforts are designed to provide economic opportunities for local businesses in other states and overseas. Still other efforts are aimed at wooing new industries and businesses.

Under the auspices of the National League of Cities (NLC), thousands of local officials descend each November on whatever city can hold their numbers, to share common experiences and to help fashion common policies between the cities and the federal government. A similar event occurs every summer for 500 mayors from around the nation. Local officials travel to Washington, D.C., every March to lobby their members of Congress, trying to refocus attention on the plight of cities.

Fred is typical of these efforts. As mayor of a large city in the South, he spent five years in a leadership position with the NLC. As chair of an important committee, he was responsible for testifying before Congress whenever relevant federal legislation was pending before either house. He chaired all of his committee meetings, doing so at least three times per year. He was responsible for shepherding his committee's priorities through Congress and was involved in the NLC's outreach program. He was rewarded for his good work by being made the president of the organization. His new position required him to visit all fifty state leagues. He received not a penny of compensation for his labor beyond the goodwill of his colleagues. Nor did his efforts assist him in seeking higher office, since he had no such ambition. After serving three terms as mayor of his city, he returned to private life, older and much more tired than when he started.

I was involved with similar responsibilities. In my role as chair of the NLC's transportation committee, I was selected by members of Congress to negotiate federal legislation involving telecommunications. The practical implication of this honor was that for nearly six months I would take the red-eye from Tucson to Washington on Friday night, negotiate in Washington on Saturday, and then take the evening flight back on Saturday night. On numerous occasions I was asked by the NLC to return to Washington to testify on pending transportation legislation. Four times per year, and then six times per year when I became a board member of the organization, I would travel to various parts of the country to convene meetings and to forge alliances with other cities around a unified approach to the federal government. Once I became mayor, these trips expanded to include the work of the Conference of Mayors as well.

While these efforts were undertaken in partnership with other cities, the bulk of my efforts revolved exclusively around my city's business. City business involves extensive travel as well, since the fate of most communities today is intertwined with both national and international currents. I led trade delegations to Europe, Asia, and Latin America. I visited Capitol Hill and the White House in search of federal grants for housing, transportation, and environmental concerns. I went to New York to help persuade the baseball commissioner to assist us in keeping major league spring training, a rich source of tourist revenue. I went back to New York to contest our bond ratings with underwriters and rating agencies. I met with the CEOs of major airlines in search of better air service. I traveled often to both coasts to persuade corporations to relocate their operations to my city.

I was not alone on these trips. Scores of cities, in jeopardy on bond ratings, send delegations to New York to argue, persuade, and cajole. The battle to relocate industries and businesses is waged by hundreds of cities, and since local economies are affected by global opportunities, city officials pursue economic opportunities globally. Once, in Central Asia, I ran into sixty-eight other American mayors pursuing economic and cultural linkages in the former Soviet Union.

Such travel is often portrayed as a perk by the media. Yet conducting city business on the road is seldom enjoyable. Travel is tiresome and boring, and the time away from home results in an overwhelming amount of work piling up while the official is absent. Jet lag and other discomforts continue to plague the traveler for days and weeks after the trip has concluded. Overseas trips are especially gruesome, involving both very long travel schedules and arduous protocol arrangements blanketing virtually every waking hour. Typically, I would take my daily jog overseas at five in the morning because that was the only time left to me.

Accommodations on the road don't live up to the "resort" image associated with travel "perks." In Mexico and Taiwan, our lodging compared well to U.S. standards. On other trips, the "beds" were actually the equivalent of small army cots. I ate my share of horsemeat and drank my fill of goat's and mare's milk (if you have a choice, take the goat's milk), and sometimes I had to use orange drinks or coffee to brush my teeth. Many nights I slept with the lights on because in the darkness the cockroaches felt free to roam at will throughout my hotel room.

Who pays for these trips? Organizations such as the National League of Cities and the Conference of Mayors do not have the funds to pay for members' travel, and city budgets do not have extensive travel allowances. In fact, the first budget category to be cut and pared is travel. Typically, my travel budget would range between $1,500 and $4,000 annually. How could I possibly take an average of ten official trips a year with such limited funds when I was 2,500 miles from Washington or New York? I could not. Table 1 illustrates a typical year's worth of travel and the pattern of payments involved for these trips. I took short trips by car. For longer trips, my office would make reservations for low-fare tickets months in advance, shopping carefully for special rates in economy class. I would pay for virtually all my meals and often for the cost of lodging. I spent roughly 10 percent of my meager salary subsidizing travel on official business, contributing about one dollar for every two dollars spent by the city for travel.

The treatment of official travel by the media and the consequent perceptions on the part of the public are often at great variance with the reality of official travel. We read of "junkets" taken by members of Congress and come to believe that these perks are typical of the trade. Locally, citizens are treated annually to the "story" of what elected officials spend on travel during the year. The story often consists of a scorecard, running from biggest to smallest spender, and focuses on either how much the travel cost the public or how often the official was out of town. In my experience, I have never seen these stories focus on the benefits of these trips to the community or the cost savings involved

TABLE I.   TRAVEL AND BUDGET EXPENSES FOR 1990

Date	Destination/Purpose	City	Out of Pocket	Other
			Paid by	
7/16–17	Santa Barbara: Telecommunications	0	$150	$177[a]
7/30–31	New York: Cable summit	0	$100	$604[b]
9/7–8	Phoenix: Urban planning conference	0	$ 75	
9/9–9	Scottsdale: NATOA conference	0	$ 70	$130[c]
10/5–8	Orlando: NLC steering committee	$565	$115	
10/31–11/1	Phoenix: City coalition strategies	$114	$ 55	
11/3–3	New York: Wooing new headquarters	$ 30	$450	
11/24–27	Atlanta: NLC Congress of Cities	$934	$106	
1/19–20	Tempe: Economic development work	0	$117	
1/25–26	Washington, D.C.: Conference of Mayors	$830	$264	
3/2–5	Washington, D.C.: Congressional Conference	$982	$210	
3/20–28	Budapest: U.S. Delegation to observe and verify first Hungarian elections	0	$200	$800[d]
4/3–3	Phoenix: Lobbying state legislators	0	$145	
5/22–25	Washington, D.C.: Lobbying on federal facilities in Tucson	0	$ 65	na[e]
6/7–8	Washington, D.C.: Meeting with Pentagon over possible base closure	$426	$110	
6/15–17	Chicago: Annual Conference of Mayors	$490	$105	

[a]California Broadcasters Association.

[b]City of New York and Conference of Mayors.

[c]National Association of Telecommunications Officers and Advisors.

[d]National Democratic Institute for International Affairs.

[e]Arizona National Guard (flight on a training aircraft).

with official travel. Whenever I returned from a trip, I filed for public inspection the costs of travel along with a statement of where I went, what I did, and what impact the trip had on the community. I can't recall a single instance in which reporters used any of this information while gathering information for the "story."

Scores of elected officials around the country struggle with the same dilemma: how to do their work effectively when they need to travel to accomplish important policy objectives and at the same time avoid the perception that they are getting something from the system that they do not deserve. When it is in the interest of the media to help fuel the cycle of mistrust toward politics and government, officials find themselves in a losing battle on this issue.

THE REAL PERKS OF OFFICE

Politicians don't run for local office for the salary, fringe benefits, or perks such as travel privileges or free lunches. All of these—and far more—can be earned from hundreds of private-sector and public-sector jobs that require less work, frustration, and personal sacrifice. The prize is the office itself: Even with its difficulties and drawbacks, winning office and keeping it are the important rewards.

Getting into office provides the ultimate benefit: an opportunity to make a difference in shaping the community, and the psychological gratification taken from having a positive impact. Winning reelection serves an equally important psychological purpose: Elections become the primary mechanism by which an incumbent can be vindicated. In most places of work, people get feedback regularly about their work performance. Public-sector employees receive feedback through written and oral evaluations. Pay raises in the private sector signify a job well done, and people receive feedback systematically even without pay increases. Salespeople can gauge from the volume of their sales how well they are doing. Supervisors often tell clerical or assembly-line workers about the quality of their work.

Political officeholders work in a different world. They know that many of the people with whom they come into contact, particularly those who wish to influence their behavior, seek to ingratiate themselves by complimenting the politician's performance. Many other citizens call because they are unhappy about what they perceive government is doing or is failing to do. This group is in no mood to provide useful feedback to the officeholder about his or her performance. Furthermore, as politics is a constant process of conflict over values and policy positions, even the most popular incumbent knows that large numbers of people will disagree with his or her policy positions. In a competitive race, winning election by 56 percent is considered a landslide; such a victory, however, means that nearly half the voters disagree with the victor. Reelection becomes the main mechanism for incumbents to demonstrate to themselves and their critics that they have done a good job.

The ultimate perk for elected officials is the receipt of privileges that allow incumbents to stay in office. Keeping the office is important not because it leads to tangible benefits but because incumbency offers opportunities to influence the course of the future, and it offers incumbents the primary mechanism by which they can feel good about what they have done in office.

A number of factors are important in allowing officials to stay in office. Of these, a critically important one is the role of money in financing elections. All elections, even municipal ones, have become exceedingly expensive, and unlike in most democracies, in America funds for campaigning are raised overwhelmingly by individual campaigns and candidates.

Campaigning in the United States has never been inexpensive. At the beginning, George Washington spent 28 gallons of rum, 50 gallons of rum punch, 34 gallons of wine, and 46 gallons of beer on 391 voters in his Fairfax County district. By the late nineteenth century, some presidential candidates were demanding and receiving a specified percentage of the assets of large corporations and banks for their campaigns.

Today, though, driven by new and expensive campaign technologies, the role of money in electoral politics has become more salient than ever before. According to the Federal Election Commission, at the end of the twentieth century candidates for the two houses of Congress spent, in non-inflationary dollars, nearly 200 percent more than in the 1970s. By 1998, at least ninety-four House candidates broke the $1 million spending barrier, while one spent $7.2 million.[18] House incumbents now are raising an average of nearly $800,000 per campaign, and if challenged, substantially more.

The story is similar in local elections. The cost for a successful mayoral campaign in a large city can run anywhere from $300,000 to $3 million every two or four years. Successful city council races in large cities typically cost between $100,000 and $300,000 every two or four years. While an incumbent member of Congress raises $25,000 to $50,000 *every month* while in office, a mayor may actually raise more. Consequently, raising money is not an activity relegated to election years. In California, for example, incumbents actually raise 60 percent of their contributions during non-election years. (While conducting a seminar on democracy and elections in the Ukraine, I shared some information on how much money is spent in the United States by candidates running for office. A member of their parliament quickly interrupted me: "I don't understand this," he said. "You people claim to be good capitalists. You say a mayor may spend the equivalent of ten times his salary to get elected. Why don't you just keep the money and not run for office?")

The extent to which campaign financing perks have been growing in politics is best illustrated by the widening gap between incumbents and challengers in raising money and spending it on elections. Twenty years ago congressional incumbents outspent challengers by an average of 35 percent. Incumbents today outraise and outspend challengers by about 300 percent. National data for local elections are not available, but the analysis of spending patterns for California jurisdictions does show a similar pattern. By the start of the 1990s, spending by incumbents dwarfed spending by challengers in California by a ratio of four to one. In larger jurisdictions such as Los Angeles and San Francisco, the incumbent's financial advantage ran as high as ten to one. The data show as well that money in local elections matters as much as money in congressional elections: Winners in medium and large jurisdictions in California typically outspent losers by a factor of three to one.

The extent to which officeholders receive fund-raising perks is actually underestimated by considering only direct contributions to campaigns, since this method fails to account for the effects of independent campaigns, campaigns that overwhelmingly favor incumbents. Typically such campaigns will spend seven times as many dollars on behalf of congressional incumbents than they will on challengers.

The fund-raising perk provided to incumbents makes life easier on the campaign trail, for at least two reasons. First, the money actually works to discourage competition or to eliminate it altogether. In some races, unchallenged incumbents at both the local and the congressional levels have been known to spend up to $1.5 million while running unopposed to discourage potentially competitive opponents in future years. For example, despite a "throw the bums out" attitude toward Congress in the 1990s, about 90 percent of incumbents who ran for reelection won. In 1994, the year of extreme anti-incumbency and a major change in the leadership of both the U.S. House and Senate, more incumbents were reelected than in 1992. In 1996, the candidate who raised the most money won 92 percent of the time, and, not surprisingly, 95 percent of incumbents running for reelection won their races.

The story is no different in local races. By 1990, incumbents in 90 percent of the state legislative contests throughout the nation ran without viable challengers. In California's state, county, and municipal elections, in large jurisdictions, "incumbents hold such a fund raising dominance that challengers rarely take them on."[19]

The flow of money into the coffers of incumbents provides a second perk: Wealthy campaigns make life far easier for incumbents on the campaign trail than for challengers. Much of the money raised by incumbents for their campaigns is not spent for direct contact with voters. Researchers found in California that only 29 cents of every dollar spent by incumbents went for direct voter contact. The majority of expenditures went for travel, consultants, and staff hired to do the work incumbents used to do when they were challengers. Challengers, who couldn't afford the luxury of overhead, spent 53 cents of every dollar on direct contact with voters, often spending sixteen-hour days working on the campaign and personally taking on tasks that incumbents delegate to paid staff and consultants.

This is the ultimate perk of office: providing a river of money for incumbents to allow them to remain in office far longer than they could with a financially level playing field. Of all the perks associated with politics, this is the one that ought to concern us the most for its negative effects on public policy and democratic governance. The huge amounts of money raised for reelection do not lead to a more informed electorate or to a better debate about public policy. Research shows that the growth of money in politics has been accompanied by a lower level of knowledge among voters about issues, and a lower level of awareness of candidates: Surveys of voters demonstrate that while spending for congressional elections has more than doubled, the percentage of voters who can successfully identify the names and party affiliations of candidates has actually decreased.

It may seem strange that more money spent on campaigns and elections results in less knowledge, but political campaigns are not like advertising to sell mouthwash or toothpaste. Most of the political dollars are spent to reduce competition, and they have the consequent effect of reducing interest in elections. No wonder, then, that the growth of campaign spending is matched by a reduction in voter turnout in both national and local races.

The flow of fund-raising perks to incumbents distorts not only the electoral process but also the way in which the policy process is pursued within the political laboratory. The burgeoning and omnipresent hunt for funds by incumbents cripples the way in which decisions are made. The vast sums contributed to reelection coffers don't come from ordinary citizens. Campaign funding perks come overwhelmingly from wealthy contributors and political action committees (PACs). Contributions from most of us are relatively insignificant—people who contribute $100 or less to congressional campaigns account for no more than 15 percent of the money raised for a campaign.

The numbers are overwhelming. In 1972, approximately 600 PACs were registered with the government; by the end of 1999, well over 4,000 PACs were active in Washington, doling out money almost exclusively to incumbents. Limited legally in their direct contributions to candidates, PACs are able to circumvent their $5,000 limits through "independent campaigns." The Realtors PAC, for example, contributed $220,000 to one Senate incumbent and over $150,000 to three House incumbents in one election year.

Attempts at reforming health care provide a good illustration of the impact of campaign contributions on public policy. In 1992 Bill Clinton was elected president in part by pledging to pursue comprehensive health-care reform. Instead of directly attacking his proposals for changes in the health-care system during the campaign, health-care insurance interests were breaking records by pouring over $41 million into the 1992 congressional campaign coffers. Evidently this was just the beginning: The flow of industry dollars to incumbents continued after the 1992 elections. Eight months later and before the introduction of health-care legislation, the Democratic Senate Campaign Committee held an "issues forum." Two hundred health industry lobbyists attended and paid the mandatory entry fee of $5,000 each. As the issue drew closer to resolution in Congress, policy makers found themselves in a "torrent of donations from the health and insurance industries. . . .

[Industry] donations increased 52 percent in the last 15 months compared to the equivalent period in the previous election cycle."[20] In a fourteen-month period, and before legislation could emerge on the floors of the Congress, 650 lobbying groups spent more than $100 million seeking to influence incumbents. The primary beneficiary on the Senate side received $611,000 in campaign contributions from health and insurance industry PACs during the period, while her House counterpart earned a hefty $540,000 for his campaign coffers between January 1993 and May 1994.

One of the possible experiments in health-care reform consists of the single-payer Canadian model of health care. The primary beneficiaries of such a plan in the United States provide virtually none of the campaign financing perks to incumbents; of course, this plan is anathema to the health insurance industry. Perhaps it is coincidental, but the single-payer option—better known, cheaper, and more cost-effective than any of the "managed competition" experiments being proposed in the congressional laboratory—received virtually no hearing in Congress.

The health-care issue is not an anomaly, and both parties are equally eager to feed at the money trough. While President Clinton was being attacked for using fund-raising perks available only in the White House, the Republicans showed that they didn't need the White House to raise cash from those who want access to power. They charged $250,000 for the privilege of sitting next to Republican leadership at major fundraisers, $100,000 for breakfast (and photo) with the House Speaker and the Senate majority leader, and $45,000 for lunch with Senate and House committee chairs.

At the local level, fund-raising perks are also much sought after and given. Studies of California's elections show that the groups affected most directly by the policies of local governments (large businesses) are by far the largest givers and are responsible for nearly two-thirds of all dollars contributed to campaigns. The evidence shows as well that these interests are contributing to the campaigns of incumbents while incumbents are making policy decisions: The largest dollar amounts contributed to campaigns come during non-election years. The comments of contributors speak for themselves. One large contributor stated, "We certainly are not going to support candidates where we have no business," while other contributors noted that their donations were "part of the cost of doing business."[21]

When it comes to fund-raising perks, local officials are not very different from their national counterparts in their hunger for fund-raising and in their willingness to diminish electoral competition. There is, however, an important difference between the two levels of politics. For over a decade, local officials have pioneered the path toward campaign finance reform. First in Seattle and Tucson, and then spreading east, local jurisdictions have engaged in fundamental campaign finance reform. No fewer than sixty local jurisdictions in California alone had enacted major changes by 1990. Critical reforms include strict disclosure provisions, strong conflict-of-interest laws, limits on the size of contributions, and in a number of jurisdictions, limits on campaign spending, with the limits accompanied by matching public funds as incentives for staying within spending limits.

Campaign finance reforms are popular with citizens who intuitively recognize the destructive effects of large sums of money on campaigns. Local officials, however, should be given substantial credit for their willingness to engage in such reforms—despite broad public support—because these changes are contrary to their interests. Incumbents who are willing to change the rules to significantly reduce campaign spending are making reelection tougher for themselves. Experiences in both Seattle and Tucson show that limits on campaign spending encourage competition, create a more level playing field between incumbents and challengers, and make campaigning more demanding and time-consuming for incumbents.

These reforms are straightforward, and this is how they work in Tucson, a jurisdiction that adopted the strategy of placing voluntary limits on spending:

- When a candidate runs for office, the candidate qualifies for public matching funds if he or she collects 200 contributions of $10 or more from local citizens for a council race and 300 contributions of $10 or more for the mayor's race.
- Once qualified, the candidate signs a legal document agreeing to limit spending to no more than the designated formula for office (29 cents per registered voter in council races and 58 cents in mayoral races, with an annual change to adjust for inflation and population change).
- The city periodically audits the campaign to assure compliance and matches every dollar raised privately by the candidate with a public dollar. At the end of the campaign, unspent public dollars are returned to the city.

Thus, half of the candidate's spending comes anonymously, from the public. Table 2 illustrates the effects of campaign finance reform in my city. Despite skyrocketing campaign costs in other jurisdictions, these reforms have substantially reduced the role of money in our municipal elections. In Tucson, the combined costs of the winning and losing mayoral campaigns are substantially below what they were in the early 1980s. Candidates may choose not to respect these limits, but then they receive no public funding, and every candidate to date who has chosen not to respect these limits has lost election, including a popular incumbent.

These figures show one more phenomenon linked to limiting spending for political campaigns. While in nearly all races without spending limits the person who raises the most wins, this is not the case in races with spending limits. Tucson's experience shows that once spending is capped, candidates who spend less can still win their races.

What the figures don't show, however, is the extent to which competition and electioneering have changed in communities that have reformed their campaign finance laws. Before campaign finance reform in my city, one person occupied the mayor's office for sixteen years. Since campaign finance reform, four new elections brought three new mayors to office. Moreover, campaigning has changed dramatically. Television advertising has been minimized, while radio advertising, coffees, rallies, and a variety of grassroots-style voter contact efforts have increased.

In contrast to campaign finance reform at the local level, reforms aimed at congressional campaigns demonstrate a history of posturing and minimal change. Campaign finance reform proposals passed the Congress during the Bush presidency with the full knowledge that the legislation would be vetoed in the White House. Once President Clinton had urged the passage of reforms, the work of federal legislators turned into a serious enterprise of trying to pass legislation that would look like fundamental change without affecting the reelection chances of incumbents. Even the boldest campaign reforms considered in the U.S. Senate in 1997 would have done little more than freeze average spending rates rather than reducing the flow of money into the hands of incumbents. Legislation passed in the House in 1994 would have voluntarily (and without substantial incentives) limited campaign spending to rates that represent more than a 50 percent *increase* over the average amount spent by incumbents.

TABLE 2.   CAMPAIGN SPENDING ON MAYORAL RACE IN TUCSON,
BEFORE AND AFTER CAMPAIGN FINANCE REFORM

Year	Candidate	Amount Spent	Total Spent by Party Nominees[a]
	Prior to Campaign Finance Reform		
1983	Incumbent (winner)	$115,032	
	Challenger	$124,954	$239,985.79
	After Campaign Finance Reform		
1987	Republican Primary:		
	Candidate (winner)	$ 43,926	
	Candidate	$ 34,914	
	Democratic Primary:		
	Candidate (winner)	$ 50,141	
	Candidate	$ 96,474	
	General Election:		
	Candidate (winner)	$ 82,216	
	Candidate	$ 91,788	$174,003.30
			($151,034.87)
1991	Republican Primary		
	Candidate (winner)	$ 15,777	
	Candidate	$ 2,704	
	Democratic Primary		
	Candidate (winner)	$ 61,228	
	Candidate	$ 34,102	
	General Election:		
	Candidate (winner)	$100,314	
	Candidate	$ 59,122	$159,435.32
			($109,372.63)
1995	Republican Primary		
	Candidate (winner)	$ 6,079	
	Democratic Primary		
	Candidate (winner)	$ 76,309	
	Candidate	$ 59,698	
	General Election		
	Candidate (winner)	$130,285	
	Candidate	$ 50,481	$188,766
			($118,368)

TABLE 2.   CONTINUED

Year	Candidate	Amount Spent	Total Spent by Party Nominees[a]
1999	Republican Primary		
	Candidate	$ 42,526	
	Democratic Primary		
	Candidate (winner)	$ 69,476	
	Candidate	$ 44,671	
	Candidate	$121,615	
	Candidate	$ 10,017	
	General Election		
	Candidate (winner)	$153,335	
	Candidate	$153,306	$306,611
			($176,883)[b]

SOURCE: Archives, City of Tucson, City Clerk's Office.

[a]Numbers in parentheses indicate constant dollars, discounted for inflation. Total figures for winning and losing candidates in the general election including spending on both primary and postprimary campaigns.

[b]In constant, noninflationary dollars, the contenders in the 1999 mayoral race spent 26 percent less than their counterparts in 1983, 16 years earlier, and before campaign finance reform.

The availability of fund-raising and other perks for politicians that enhance electoral success constitutes nothing new in politics. We have a long and sordid history of intimate linkages between those in political power and those with economic power in both city hall and Capitol Hill. The introduction of civil service reforms in America's cities at the turn of the twentieth century came in response to parties and candidates using public jobs to secure the backing of campaign supporters. Other questionable practices have stimulated efforts at reform over the past hundred years. The irony reflected in the history of these reforms, however, is that while they led to cleaner politics, the legal exchange of money for elections has made incumbency safer and has allowed the fund-raising perk to become an intrusive and destructive influence on the nation's political laboratories.

There is a simple answer to this problem: strict limits on campaign spending, matched by substantial public financing of elections. The work in the political laboratory will continue to diminish in value without this change. Experiments cannot be conducted when the experimenters are being paid off to avoid conducting many crucial experiments. Voters cannot exchange one group of people in the laboratory for another when the river of money flowing through the election cycle blocks the public's view of who is available to replace incumbents.

Public anger and outrage at this state of affairs should be enough to overcome the personal interests of incumbents in holding on to the status quo. Public outrage over Watergate led to major changes in campaign practices, but there is no such outrage today even though the flow of money is stronger and the advantages of incumbency are greater. Perhaps anger and outrage would intensify with fewer stories about junkets and more stories on the linkages between campaign contributions and the voting records of our members of Congress. Perhaps the decision makers in the media believe that the public won't care. If people are increasingly willing to believe that the laboratory is not important or that its defects cannot be fixed, then why should they be outraged about the effects of campaign funding on their political laboratory? Aren't all politicians a bit like former congressman Rostenkowski, who lifted thousands of dollars from the office stamp fund? If so, then who cares if competition for office is unfair?

There is a Catch-22 here. If the political laboratory is going to work well, fundamental campaign finance reforms are needed. Such changes will not happen unless voters force incumbents to surrender practices that benefit only them. Yet voters will not see these reforms as crucial unless they begin to empathize more with people in the political laboratory: to understand that even well-meaning men and women in office are caught in a process that is neither well-meaning nor likely to benefit most citizens.

Meanwhile, all is not bleak. We don't need to look far if we want to find elected officials who work for minimal wages, sacrifice personal gain for public service, and change the political rules at their own peril to bring added competition to elections. We can find these people in our own community. It is in the local political laboratory where there is promise of gaining greater empathy toward both the process of making policy and the people engaged in it. Local politics, often sleazier than national politics throughout our history, has changed in fundamental ways.

For a civic culture in decline, it is understandable that media scrutiny and public anger are directed at politicians who reach for the perks of office. Yet if these people are different at the local level, how can we learn about them? The answer lies in the proximity of local government to its citizens. In our communities and our neighborhoods, voluntary organizations blossom everywhere. Some organizations (such as neighborhood associations and business groups) defend their turf against the encroachment of government experiments, while others (environmental groups, consumer organizations, and advocates for minorities, women, and the disabled) advocate changes in the experiments being conducted. Although traditional sources of association (such as the PTA, the Boy Scouts and Girl Scouts, and, yes, even bowling leagues) are shrinking, at least some evidence seems to suggest that alternative organizations are springing up to take their place.

Collaborative activity among citizens and between citizens and their government doesn't mushroom by itself. It must be nurtured if it is to survive. Sadly, as these organizations blossom, the actual numbers of citizens involved with them are decreasing as cynicism and distrust tear through the fabric of grassroots democracy in our communities. Nevertheless, the seeds of a stronger civic culture lie in the success of these organizations. Citizens, through these organizations and even as individuals, have direct access to public officials in ways impossible to attain at the state or national level. Their positive experiences with the political laboratory can serve to reenlist those citizens who are dropping out. Direct personal experience with elected officials at the local level exposes activists to the reality of working conditions for those who labor in the political laboratory. Citizens who make contact with local officials usually come away from the experience impressed with how hard their representatives work and how extensive their commitments are to their jobs. Direct contacts enhance empathy toward officials and the work being conducted in the political laboratory. These contacts function to help re-create trust in the democratic process of governance.

Through proximity with the men and women who fashion policies in the local laboratory, opinion leaders from the public—and the people whom they influence—can develop greater empathy toward the democratic process. It is then that the search for evil in the laboratory can be replaced by the search for the best scientists and better experiments. At the municipal level the task is easier, and the roadblocks are fewer.

5

A WEEK IN THE LIFE

"If you haven't been bummed out yet watching C-SPAN . . . watching your congressman pretending to work . . . then listen to this."[22]

What takes up the time of officeholders? Do they sit in plush rooms, sealed behind thick wooden doors, trading votes? Or, as they say on talk radio, do they really spend "most of their time trying to figure out how to pick our pockets"? At the local level, the answer is closer to a reality few of us see: Local officeholders work long, hard hours struggling to respond to the needs of constituents and trying to fashion policies that will address urban problems meaningfully. Unsurprisingly, the public seldom sees this view of politicians. The media do not track their everyday lives. The vast majority of citizens, by whose grace they serve, never have direct contact with them. Citizens, through the media, see them at their worst, and politicians try to have the public see them at their best, but they are seldom seen at their typical daily work. Consequently, our ability to empathize with what they do and how they do it is virtually nonexistent.

The chronology below outlines a week in the life of a mayor involved with governing the thirtieth largest city in the nation. The styles of mayors and the problems of their cities are unique in many respects. Neither is *any* week typical in the true sense of the word. Each week brings, along with the routine, a bewildering array of new problems and challenges. Still, the week described here is typical in the sense that it conveys how political time is normally spent. I checked this schedule with a number of mayors of other cities. While the specifics involving places, dates, and issues vary greatly from city to city, they saw nothing unusual in the general flow and volume of events.

WEDNESDAY

Wednesday is the hardest day of the week. We are recovering from the fallout of Monday's legislative agenda while planning for next Monday's council deliberations. Room must be found between these two events for virtually everything else.

6:00 A.M.

I'm on the road, jogging. Each day I vary my route, running through different neighborhoods and arterial streets to reduce the boredom, and by assuring myself that I am also inspecting aspects of our city, I feel less guilty about taking an hour away from work.

Sometimes I don't have to feel guilty. Last month, as I rounded the corner on a main thoroughfare, a citizen joined me, dressed in suit and wingtip shoes. He asked if he could jog with me for a while, and before I could decline his offer, he joined me and began to talk about his issues with the city. After three blocks, his suit was soaked with sweat. At the seventh block, he asked if he could make an appointment to come see me. Only when I agreed did he stop jogging. As I turned the corner I saw him sitting on a bus bench, carefully removing his shoes and massaging his feet.

7:30 A.M.

The board of directors of our economic development agency is meeting. Sitting at the table and arguing politely are business leaders who mistrust government and government leaders who keep a wary eye on the business representatives. I created this group, and I studiously attend all the meetings. With limited funds, large egos in conflict, and an economy in recession, we work to bring new industries into the community and to prop up the businesses we have. Before this organization, sixteen different agencies did the same job, and they seldom talked to one another. Now we are doing better.

8:45 A.M.

I sneak out of the meeting and race over to city hall where I present a proclamation for spinal health month. The poster child who takes the proclamation is an adorable six-year-old girl in a wheelchair, adorned with ribbons and bows.

9:00 A.M.

I manage to get out of the office before my guests do, and run down the stairs. (The elevators take forever. A previous council, trying to save money, eliminated one of the elevators. Now we spend tens of thousands of dollars' worth of time waiting.) My destination is just across the street, where I chair the meeting of our metropolitan Council of Governments. This organization, representing all of the jurisdictions in the region, coordinates policies and develops a common response to federal and state mandates. That is what it is supposed to do. In practice, it is an organization where jurisdictions denounce one another over territorial disputes and work together only when they are in jeopardy of losing federal funding.

The place is a minefield of contending egos and clashing interests. Knowing this, the participants conspire to get through the agenda as fast as possible. The record for the shortest meeting is three minutes. We won't set a new record today. We need to agree on water-contamination issues, on a transportation program, on a process for land-use planning, and on a response to a state legislature that is intent on imposing higher taxes on us. Fortunately, our respective bureaucracies had spent the previous week trying to come to some tentative agreement on all of these issues, and we have been briefed well. We come to agreement with minimum acrimony and leave before we have a chance to pick fights with each other. Nevertheless, the meeting took longer than expected.

10:15 A.M.

As I rush back to city hall, I find myself behind schedule. Two groups are waiting for me: One is from a neighborhood association; the other group consists of a developer with his entourage, intent on building a multistory apartment complex. The two groups sit as far away from each other as the size of the waiting area permits, and they chat in conspiratorial tones. Each group spends twenty minutes with me, presenting the best case they can for their side. I ask questions but refuse to accede to their requests to tell them how I plan to vote. I simply don't have enough information yet, but I sketch out my general concerns. They will have to wait for my decision until after the public hearing on the matter.

11:00 A.M.

I meet with the director of a local theater company. He was delegated by the city's arts organizations to argue for a larger share of public resources. He catches me in a difficult dilemma. I supported past efforts for public arts funding. Now, however, resources are scarce, and every new dollar going to the arts will have an impact on other, more basic services. I need to say no without damaging what we have built so far. My job is to show enough support to motivate our arts organizations to do more with less and not to lose the momentum we have developed. When he leaves I realize that I have no idea whether I've succeeded. My exec walks in, smiles, and says: "Keep going . . . you're doing fine!"

11:30 A.M.

I walk into my secretary's office and grab my messages, frowning at the size of the pile. There must be at least fifty messages for me since the office opened today. As the calls came in, my secretary tried to sort them according to the needs of the caller. Some went to my exec and others to two aides working on various areas of constituent concerns. I get the messages when the caller refuses to talk to my staff or when my secretary can't figure out who should get the message (I'm the default option) or if the call is from another elected official or department head who needs to talk to me. In addition, when someone is calling about one of my decisions, I want to respond directly. Finally, I'm working on specific policy areas, and I want my office to funnel public concerns on those issues to me.

The telephone messages cover a rich range of community life: problems with our city cable franchise; concerns about timely police response; garbage that was not picked up yesterday; complaints about the lack of efficiency in city court. Several developers call about their zoning cases. Three people want to voice their feelings about drunk driving. Two people call about job training programs. Representatives of social service agencies want to see me about funding for programs for the homeless. Some people are calling to demand a leash law for cats (and there are calls from citizens denouncing the idea of a cat leash law). A couple of people phone to express their support for consolidating governments. Three people call to demand an end to annexations by the city. Several callers want to complain about not getting cheap airfares to the West Coast. One person leaves a message asking for a job.

Two calls are logged about our recycling program. Three people phone to denounce the Women's Commission for its support of lesbians. My spouse is calling to see how things are going.

I answer my spouse's call first. Then I start returning other calls on the basis of whoever called first. I take notes while chatting with people, some to myself about the relevance of the call to upcoming legislation, others as reminders to my exec to follow through on commitments I am making. I manage to get through five phone calls before my next appointment appears.

NOON

This meeting takes me into uncharted territory. I'm getting involved with the politics of baseball since we are in the midst of a baseball/tourism crisis. Our city hosts major-league spring training, an activity that is the closest thing to having our own major league team, and spring training is a great joy for many of our citizens. Spring training also generates much tourist revenue as people from around the nation use their baseball loyalties as an excuse to flock to the Southwest while the weather is still miserable elsewhere. Recently, the owners of our spring training team—after a forty-five-year association with our city—informed us that they have received a better offer from Florida and will be leaving. We are searching for a replacement that will not involve mortgaging the future. This meeting with key business leaders, former major league players living here, and the parks department will generate a strategy that will unite us with the governor, the commissioner of baseball, tourist interests, and economic development specialists. We will find another team, but right now we are all doom and gloom.

1:00 P.M.

I go back to returning my phone messages. Meanwhile, my secretary brings in my mail "log," a list of the day's mail, followed by the mail itself. I peruse the mail log while I'm on the phone, making notes in the margin. This is a weeding process: Some letters I redirect to my staff, and others I set aside for myself. After culling, I still have twenty pieces of mail to handle directly. By the time my next appointment arrives, I've answered four more phone messages.

1:30 P.M.

"Before you get the next one . . . " is my exec's favorite phrase. As I'm about to get to my next appointment, she hurls herself through the door saying it, indicating that something important needs my attention. I promise her that I will get to it soon.

1:32 P.M.

Mr. Smith made an appointment four weeks ago to see me. This was the earliest date available. He is clearly agitated, and as my secretary shows him in, she gives me one of those knowing looks that says: "I can have the cops here in a couple of minutes." She is both a secretary and a cop at an intersection constantly on the brink of gridlock.

Mr. Smith is angry about city court. He paid his seventh traffic ticket but the computer mistakenly issued a summons for his arrest. When he subsequently ran a stop sign and got caught, the police carted him off to jail. As he tells the story, his complaints stretch to cover police practices, water rates, rush-hour traffic, and his problems at home. I have suddenly shifted from being a mayor to being a counselor. By the time my secretary looks in to tell me my next appointment has arrived, Mr. Smith is calmer and I've promised him that I will do something concrete about the computer running amok. He leaves smiling and on his way out stops to praise my secretary for her attentiveness to him.

2:00 P.M.

"Before you get the next one . . . ," my exec says to me again, but this time she is not smiling. I get the point and stop. There is a television news crew waiting for me in the hallway. A particularly nasty member of the county's board of supervisors just denounced me at their meeting, claiming that I falsely took credit for bringing into the community a major new business, and he threatens to disrupt our economic development efforts. Reporters are here for conflict and drama, and want a response. I can tell them that he's an idiot (he is); I can spend the next ten minutes explaining what my role was in recruiting the company; or I can ignore the television news reporters long enough so they will miss their deadlines and will be forced to run a small story or no story at all.

I can't ignore them. I could spend all my time meeting with people and I still couldn't communicate directly with as many citizens as I can through a minute on the evening news or three paragraphs on the front page. Knowing this, I have developed a simple law of the press: Never say no when they call. For television, I confine my remarks to short statements that can be easily used for the broadcast. For newspaper reporters, I will sit for interviews whenever they ask me and for as long as they need to ask questions, and I know that I can mislead them only once or twice before my credibility is lost . . . so I know I can't mislead them.

These procedures are not easy to follow. It is extremely difficult to say something in thirty seconds. I ache to grab control of the microphone and tell the story in its full complexity. There are times when I would rather run and hide when I know the news will anger or depress people. But the procedures I developed for myself are worth following. Even before I became mayor I received more airtime and more coverage on the news than my colleagues by simply following these basic rules. The extra airtime allowed me time to try to convey to the public what was going on, and to marshal public support for my positions to a degree that others could not. However, I don't have the luxury of hiding from the difficult stories and "bad" news.

Today is not a fun news day. My exec ushers in the press. I am now facing cameras and reporters from three different television stations and one reporter from a radio news program. Reporters from the two newspapers have left messages asking me to call them back. The process is very efficient: The television reporters ask if I know what the story is about while the camera crews set up microphones and station their cameras. We joke and make small talk in order to "warm up." Once the cameras are rolling, each reporter asks a question in turn, and I try not to give the same response each time. Satisfied, they leave within twenty minutes. The calls to the newspaper reporters take much longer, and I'm careful to avoid alienating the county while denouncing the errant supervisor. I am trying to convey two messages. One is that the supervisor conducting the attack is a belligerent, obnoxious fellow who is envious when others are successful. The second is that he missed the point—it's not who gets credit for bringing in jobs, it's getting the jobs to the community that is important.

I won't have time to see how the story actually airs on the evening news, but my spouse will tell me when I get home. While I'm working with the media, my next appointment patiently sits in the outer office, impressed by the flow of television equipment around her.

3:00 P.M.
I go back to the "routine," although now I'm behind by nearly an hour. The person who has waited for me has a life as hectic as mine, and for

the fifth time that day I apologize for being late. This time we are focusing on economic conversion: how to save thousands of defense-related jobs in our community that are disappearing after the end of the cold war. These jobs pay good wages, and too often they are replaced by jobs paying far less. My meeting is with a veteran of economic conversion efforts. She fears that our economic development strategy is paying insufficient attention to the problem. I agree, and we try to develop an approach we can use to inject more of this focus. She leaves looking confident, but I'm a bit more somber. I don't know any good models around the nation that had success in saving more than a fraction of these jobs.

3:30 P.M.
I get time to answer a few more phone calls.

3:45 P.M.
This meeting is with a group of businesspeople who are angry with the city about a new public recreation facility. They feel that their own businesses will be negatively affected by "unfair" government competition. One of them wishes to engage in debate about the "inherent corruptness of government," and another wants to discuss what constitutes "essential and public services." I get trapped into their arguments, and we debate needlessly about whether recreational facilities are an appropriate public activity. By the time I've come to my senses, we have escalated to a no-win situation. Getting my second wind, I confront them with the fact that these facilities are financed with bonds authorized by the public for this purpose. I try to help by indicating that while I will not support their position, I would be willing to discuss what should be the range of activities inside the new facility. They are not happy, and neither am I, but we conclude the meeting by agreeing to review the matter publicly at a council meeting.

4:40 P.M.
My "agenda books" arrive for next Monday's council meeting. These books identify each item for the city council's formal meeting and provide vital information on each, including pertinent data on the costs of each action and the consequences of alternative policy choices. Monday's meeting takes up two thick books.

I meet with my staff to talk about how we will handle the agenda. As we run through items, they tell me how their work with constituents relates to these issues, where policies seem to be working and where they are not, and where the city's administration has or has not responded to our inquiries. I take notes and parcel out work for each of them, including requests for additional information not covered in the agenda books. We agree to meet again on Friday to talk about what else will be needed for the meeting.

5:45 P.M.
After everyone else leaves, my exec and I talk about the feedback she has received from council offices regarding the agenda. To iron out any potential conflicts, we agree on a list of council members I need to talk to before the meeting. We must be the last ones leaving city hall—the elevator appears immediately.

6:15 P.M.
I'm on my way to have a drink with a friend to talk about the development of a task force on children and mental health. On the way to the restaurant, I return phone calls from the car to those I can reach at home. I'm disturbing them during the dinner hour, but they are impressed that I'm still working.

6:45 P.M.
We have a drink and talk about creating a task force. I learn quickly that the mental health community is divided on the issue at hand, and we develop a strategy to include the competing factions in the task force. I threaten to ditch the project unless my friend can enlist the help of every major group involved with the conflict. She concurs.

7:45 P.M.
I drive home, making more phone calls on the way.

8:00 P.M.
It's great to be home. My spouse and I chat a bit about her day, but she realizes that I'm distracted and asks me about mine. The phone starts to ring. We agree not to answer it.

8:45 P.M.
I need to run out for a "minute." A wonderful group of volunteers is sitting in an office, stitching together teddy bears they will donate to victims of domestic violence. It has been six months since they asked me to come by and say hello, and they are offended that I haven't done so. Now, they are thrilled to see me. I'm moved by their tender care in

sewing the bears, as if by osmosis they will be able to pass on some tenderness to those souls who will need it later.

10:15 P.M.

I'm home again, just in time to say "good night" to my spouse, who is falling asleep. She tells me that the news reported my comments and that I "looked good." I grab a sandwich, sit down with a tape recorder, and answer the mail I brought home from the office.

11:20 P.M.

The mail is done. It's time to make a list of uncompleted tasks I need to finish in the next couple of days, including answering the phone messages piling up on the home phone's machine. I try to organize the remainder of the week.

MIDNIGHT

I'm exhausted, yet still "wired." I turn on the television, and while some sitcom rerun plays on, I sit worrying about how the morning paper will play the story of charges and countercharges over our economic development efforts.

THURSDAY

5:30 A.M.

I grab the newspaper from the front porch, stomach churning, and walk back into the house. The story is not great, written by a reporter whose beat is county government and who is used to constant wrangling there. He treats the story as "typical bickering" between governments. I decide to shake it off by going for a run. My spouse is already at work by the time I get back.

7:00 A.M.

I'm on my way to my university office. Tuesdays and Thursdays are "reserved" for my other job. These are the days I teach and do research. Substituting the professorial hat for the mayoral one is a bit like going back into the womb. Compared to city hall, the university is a gentle, loving place. Students are interested in learning, not in seeking political advantage. My colleagues in the department expect no more and no less from me than from themselves, and their professional successes don't depend on a constant questioning of my behavior. I love going to the university.

I try to insulate my activities on campus from my activities downtown. The people in my downtown office know that they should call me at school only when there is an emergency, although we are still negotiating about what that means. City bureaucrats know better than to call here. Even the media are apologetic when they call, although they are a bit more brazen about it. Fortunately, most citizens forget that I hold a job outside of city hall, and fewer of them call me at the university than at home.

7:20 A.M.

I prepare for my first class, a course on international politics. I don't teach courses on local government, and the change in focus between politics and academia keeps me fresh in both jobs.

10:00 A.M.

The focus in class today is on defense policy. As I walk in, one student smiles and says, "I saw you on the news last night." "Occupational hazard," I mutter. For the next seventy minutes we discuss the changing landscape of defense policy, and not a word is heard about local issues. Even the issue of economic conversion is discussed in an international context. The students are interested and responsive and I'm almost beaming as we leave class.

11:25 A.M.

On the way back to my office, I find six messages, three from my office and three from the media.

11:30 A.M.

Office hours: I see a number of students, including undergraduates (some needing academic advice, others who want to chat about exams) and three graduate students who are working on a research project with me. The phone rings five times; I don't answer it.

1:30 P.M.

Office hours are over. I read through my notes for my next class, and to sharpen my focus I reread one of the articles I assigned for today. Then I call my exec, who is patiently waiting for me to return her call.

3:00 P.M.

I start teaching my second class. This one is on mass media and political culture. The subject begins to skirt perilously close to local government, and I struggle to keep it at bay.

4:30 P.M.

My exec calls again. Will I do a live shot on the news at five o'clock? The remote truck will be waiting for me in front of my office. I agree, return a couple of additional calls, brush the chalk dust off my dark pants, and go out to meet the reporter and camera crew.

6:00 P.M.

I keep an all-purpose jacket at my university office. I grab it while I run out to a hotel where 300 people are welcoming the deputy secretary of defense. I take the first ten minutes, saying something that I hope sounds meaningful about economic conversion, and present him with an honorary citizenship from our city. I sneak out before his remarks are concluded.

7:00 P.M.

It's poker night. For the last fourteen years, on every other Thursday, seven of us get together to play poker. This event is sacred, something like a cross between a family gathering and therapy. Only my spouse calls here for me, and she does so only to relay calls when they are of an emergency nature. The rules are simple on poker night: We talk about cards and about light moments in our lives, and watch college basketball when the University of Arizona is playing. We never, ever talk about politics. It is the only place besides my home where I feel completely free. I used to think that the game was my little secret until one day a police sergeant explained to me that he used to cruise my friend's house on Thursday nights, keeping an eye on us.

FRIDAY

6:00 A.M.

I don't have time to run today. I read my agenda books before I leave for work, taking notes on what seems murky in the staff analysis and writing down questions I need answered.

8:00 A.M.

I write an outline for a brief speech I will be giving in an hour.

8:30 A.M.

On the way to my first appointment, I call the office from the car and ask my secretary to run through my messages from Thursday. We talk about which of these should be redirected to others and which can wait until I get back to city hall.

9:00 A.M.

A state organization is meeting in Tucson. Their focus is on bilingual education. I give opening remarks and talk about my own bilingualism as my window on understanding American culture, and about the pride I take in the great cultural diversity of our community. I'm done by 9:30, after the organizers have solicited a public commitment from me to continue supporting language programs in government and education.

9:30 A.M.

I return a couple of phone calls while driving back to the office. My spouse calls on my car phone. Our chat feels like the proverbial oasis in the middle of the desert.

10:00 A.M.

We are holding a staff conference in my office to discuss Monday's council meeting. My exec reports on which council members are opposed to our initiatives. We talk about pending "craziness": anyone around the council table who would be willing to raise issues designed to make the city look foolish or the administration unprepared. I ask my staff to gather additional information for me on three items for Monday's meeting. On the way out, I glance at my new, bulging mail log and my secretary stuffs new phone messages in my shirt pocket.

11:00 A.M.

The weekly "caucus" is starting across the hall. According to the state's open-meetings law, a majority of the council can meet to discuss and decide issues only if the meeting is advertised in advance and the meeting is held in public. Closed caucuses, however, can be held by members of the same political party. In order to guarantee that we can never come to a conclusion behind closed doors, our caucus of Democratic members of the city council never holds more than three elected officials (four is a majority). We use these occasions to talk about problems we are having with issues coming before us. Council aides usually sit in for caucus members who are not there, and they take notes and offer (ever so politely) suggestions. There is just enough airing of concerns at these sessions to allow us to come to a better understanding of how members of the governing body view upcoming problems and legislation. At times we leave these sessions more confused than when we came in, but often they allow us a bit more empathy toward one another. Without these caucuses, Monday's meetings would be utter, unending chaos.

12:15 P.M.

I hurry to a restaurant two blocks from city hall to meet with the presiding judge of the superior court and the chief justice of the state supreme court. I'm trying to give them our city's magistrates. We are not equipped to run city court, and we are too involved with it to be able to respect the principle of separation of powers. The judges I lunch with are honorable, caring people, and they understand my position. They don't want the additional hassles but agree to work on a structure for consolidating local courts in the region. Now, all I need to do is to sell the idea to the city council.

1:45 P.M.

I'm back in the office, meeting with the city manager. We develop a strategy for enticing a large firm to move its manufacturing to Tucson. My phone messages are still in my breast pocket; the mail log is still sitting on my desk, unopened.

3:00 P.M.

I spend the next hour calling five of our council members. We chat about their day and their concerns about Monday's meeting. I share with them the conversation about the potential new firm, and I press them for their support on three issues of great importance (to me) on Monday's agenda. I get one firm commitment and one hesitant no, but I sense that each of them is pleased that I called.

4:00 P.M.

My next appointment is here: four people from the city's south side, angry about a local health danger. The city discovered that there was illegal dumping of trichloroethylene (TCE) in the aquifer decades ago. In this particular neighborhood there seems to be a higher than normal rate of some rare cancers, and the neighbors are greatly worried. We agree to speed the cleanup by threatening the Environmental Protection Agency, holding the offending party responsible, and pressing the state to provide additional health services. My exec takes notes, making sure that honoring any commitments I make will not have to depend on my terrible memory.

4:45 P.M.

My last appointment is with the fire chief and a lawyer (with client) who wants to prove that the city's paramedic program stinks and is too expensive whereas his client's private program is cost-effective. He wants a contract from the city and implies that he can get the state to force the city to hire a private contractor. As the lawyer makes his case, I find myself staring at the fire chief, hoping through sheer eye contact that I can keep him from exploding in anger. I fail. The eruption is not pretty, and I intervene to calm down everyone. Then it's my turn. I point out that our paramedic program is one of the most professional and well-liked programs in the city. I suggest that four members of the governing body may wish to change our present policy, but they will do so over my dead body. The chief is relieved, the lawyer is not pleased, and I'm trying to make happy small talk as I usher everyone out of my office. As I head out toward my car, I grab another batch of mail from my desk and stuff it into my briefcase.

6:00 P.M.

We are holding a reception at the air base. This facility contributes hundreds of millions of dollars annually to the local economy, but now it has been placed on a "possible closure list" by the Pentagon. The purpose of the reception is to convey to the base commander that we love him and his mission. Once that is done, several of us huddle to plan the meeting with our congressional delegation and Pentagon officials. Ultimately we will succeed, but at this moment we are uncertain about our prospects.

7:30 P.M.

I come home to change and shower. My spouse and I will be together tonight, but not alone.

8:20 P.M.

We are at the annual NAACP dinner. We sit at a table on top of a riser, overlooking fifty tables of guests. We sit together because the organizers know that we won't let them separate us. Our hosts are gracious and friendly, and my spouse is incredibly helpful by doing most of my small talk as well as hers. I nibble at my dinner while thinking of something to say that is both witty and important when it is my turn to speak. There is so much to talk about: issues of economic and social justice, and the challenges facing our collective future. Then my host whispers to me:

"Please keep your comments light and short." Suddenly, I want to go home and curl up in bed.

11:15 P.M.

We were promised that the dinner would take two hours. So far, each speaker managed to talk twice as long as requested (including me). My spouse comforts me with the thought that the night can't go on forever.

SATURDAY

6:30 A.M.

This is the perfect time to get a haircut. The person who cuts my hair is actually willing to get up this early on a Saturday morning. Bless her!

7:15 A.M.

I'm driving to Phoenix, 110 miles from Tucson, to meet with my counterparts. The drive is boring, but it gives me an opportunity to organize my thoughts about Monday's meeting. I scribble notes while the car is on cruise control.

9:30 A.M.

We meet about recycling. We want to create markets for a fledgling recycling industry. Six cities are collaborating on a pilot project that is part economic development, part environmental conservation. We are trying to figure out what to do with recyclable materials. We feel like pioneers exploring new terrain.

11:30 A.M.

Driving home, I get to return more phone calls.

3:00 P.M.

My spouse and I go to the city zoo. Our seven sister-city committees are holding a festival and fund-raising event. I'm here to reinforce the efforts of good citizens who have given generously of their time. I chat with folks at each of the booths, sample each national food, and plot a little strategy about upcoming sister-city events.

5:00 P.M.

We head over to the University of Arizona's football game. There are tens of thousands of people here who want to shake my hand, ask a question or two about the city, or complain about something that is important in their lives. At halftime, we go to the president's box, where assorted political figures are continuing to conduct city, county, state, and federal business. Even the game is exciting; in character, the team is an underdog today and so manages to win.

9:00 P.M.
We walk home, knowing that the rest of the evening is ours.

SUNDAY

8:00 A.M.
After breakfast, I start working on the mail I brought home. Part of the dictation consists of letters that need to be sent out; part of it is direction to my staff to follow through on various problems identified in the correspondence.

10:00 A.M.
I call four of our council members, using information about the air base closure as the pretext for my call. During the conversations we drift toward Monday's agenda, and I wait for further objections regarding my initiatives. Hearing none, I'm beginning to convince myself that the legislative session will go smoothly.

11:15 A.M.
I'm at a charity bowling tournament and I bowl with a pro-am team. The cause is a good one and I enjoy bowling. When the television news crew comes over to "shoot video," I bowl two strikes in a row. I'm denounced by the pros for being a "money bowler." Clearly, politicians are competitive people. I win a trophy for having the highest amateur score, and I feel like I've won the lottery.

1:45 P.M.
Back home, constituents are calling. A controversial zoning issue will come before the council on Monday, and while I was bowling, both the neighborhood association and the developer have left messages.

2:15 P.M.
We go to my spouse's annual company picnic. If I skip this one, I'm dead meat at home.

4:00 P.M.
I arrive at a television studio for a half-hour interview. The program focuses on minorities in our community. Today's subject is police/

minority relations. I tell the viewers of my pride in our police force. The chief is Hispanic, we have an aggressive program to recruit minorities and women, and our officers are well trained. We argue about paying officers for bilingual skills. The show goes well.

5:00 P.M.

It's time to relax. We watch the end of a football game on television. My Giants are losing again.

7:00 P.M.

My spouse and I are supposed to go to a dinner honoring volunteers. I can't find the energy to go out again. I call my exec and ask if she would go and represent me. Clearly she is not happy about this, but she was going to go anyway. We spend the rest of the evening at home. After my spouse falls asleep, I grade essay exams piling up in the office.

2:00 A.M.

The phone is ringing. I know this isn't a constituent call. Citizens rarely call in the middle of the night; it's more likely to be a call from the police. We have a policy of civilian oversight on police shootings. If an officer shoots a citizen during a police emergency, a shooting board is convened, and one member of the city council, by rotation, will go out to the scene and sit on the shooting board. I've done my share of this duty, and I usually get called in the middle of the night. Going out to a scene at two o'clock in the morning, looking at bone fragments lying in dried blood, staring into the eyes of a shaken officer who is second-guessing himself over a split-second decision . . . none of this is spelled out in my job description.

Fortunately, tonight's call is a wrong number. Grumpy but relieved, I fall asleep.

MONDAY

6:00 A.M.

Mondays are the days when reporters sharpen their pencils, bureaucrats take stomach medication, spouses of elected officials prepare for long evenings, and parking spaces are at a premium near city hall. The city council is in session on Monday. Going for a long run today is imperative.

8:00 A.M.

I meet with my exec about new developments over the weekend. I want as few surprises as possible. I ask her to call a couple of council aides and to follow up on additional information that could sway their bosses. She shares with me new data generated by her and by some of the city's departments since Friday morning. I call the most intransigent council member at his house, trying to minimize his opposition. He seems to be more unhappy than usual.

9:15 A.M.

I race over to a new facility we are opening. It came to us after we wooed it away from scores of cities bidding for the project. It will employ several hundred people in our city, at wages much lower than we need, but they are the best jobs we could find at the moment. This is the time for an uplifting speech to give thanks to the people who were involved in the effort and then cutting the ribbon. While introducing me, one of our local businesspeople gives me a backhanded compliment by pointing out that this must be a special event because I don't cut many ribbons. He is correct. My predecessor spent a huge chunk of his time cutting ribbons for new businesses. I average about twenty invitations a week to do the same, but I refuse to do more than one or two, and then only for businesses that are new and not in competition with others. I learned early on that each of these symbolic events takes precious time away from policy making and constituent activities.

When it's my turn to speak, I joke about my ribbon-cutting shortcomings since the official city cloning machine broke last year. People laugh, but the joke isn't funny and I sense that they have no idea how little time there is in my life. Perhaps they don't care. Perhaps they think that ribbon cutting is very important. I lose votes and support by making these choices. I get a sudden urge to talk to them about the life of a mayor, but it would be inappropriate. I cut the ribbon, shake hands, and hustle back to the office.

10:30 A.M.

The phone messages have backed up again. I ignore all but the ones from council members. My first appointment is here. We discuss a project to provide social programs to troubled teenagers (most of our teenagers seem to be troubled). The project will require bringing together social service agencies, the city's parks and recreation department, school districts, parents, and people from the private sector. We outline our goals, create a timetable, and assign tasks.

11:15 A.M.
Martha is calling. She is a news producer at one of our local television stations. She calls most Mondays around this time, asking the same question: "What's news?" She is asking me what I consider to be the most newsworthy item for today's meeting. The city council meeting is too long to have a news crew sit through the whole session. The news producer needs to know when the camera crew should show for the meeting, when to "shoot," and on what issues to interview the "two sides to the story." I run through a short list of issues, knowing which ones are bound to generate the most controversy, and I sprinkle it with issues that may show little "drama" but are important (I believe) to the community. She asks if I will be available during one of the breaks. We set up a time to meet her crew outside of chambers.

NOON
I'm at a press conference called to unveil a historical facility on the site of the founding of our city. The organizers of this event have worked closely with city hall to find a way to remind people of the historical character of a city in the midst of perpetual change. Their timing today is horrible—on Monday they vie for attention with the city council. Their efforts will bear little fruit.

1:00 P.M.
Back to my phone messages: I make three calls while skimming through the new mail log.

1:30 P.M.
Study session begins. The agenda committee created an agenda that is, in theory, both timely and manageable. Timelines are gauged by the committee's guesses about how long the discussions should take, which is determined by the issue's salience, complexity, and the overall controversy surrounding it. Study session is expected to run three hours. Today we will run one and a half hours beyond our deadline.

6:00 P.M.
As the study session ends, my exec and I drive over to the Mexican consulate. The consul is holding a reception honoring Hispanics, but no function seems to have a single purpose. My presence is requested in

part to chat about further linkages between the city and the Republic of Mexico. We agree to exchange business groups with Guadalajara and to explore various trade relationships.

7:00 P.M.

We grab sandwiches on the way back to city hall, and I call my spouse from the car. She wants to know when I'll get home, but her guess is as good as mine: The experience with the study session does not bode well for an efficient evening meeting. Once back in the office, my exec and I munch on our sandwiches and discuss the follow-up work the office will need to do in light of the decisions made at study session.

7:30 P.M.

The "regular" meeting of the city council is beginning. Every hour we take a ten-minute break to shake the cobwebs out of our heads, to use the bathrooms, and to chat with our staffs. By midnight, most citizens are gone. The only people left—besides the council and key city staff—are three sleepy members of the cable television crew (we are seen live on a local station), two tired and grumpy reporters from the news-papers, and one bored police officer, dressed in a T-shirt, jeans, and running shoes (she's undercover, there to protect us).

The long day has taken its toll. The elected officials are very tired, and fortunately they know better than to do anything significant this late in the evening. The reporters are on the "death watch": They know that nothing will happen now, but they can't afford to leave in case someone comes in and shoots one of us, which is why the undercover cop sits in the audience. She looks asleep but I know she is awake. One late Mon-day night a scruffy-looking citizen straggled to the microphone after midnight, started yelling at the governing body, and then reached into a large brown paper bag he was carrying. As we froze on the dais, I saw the undercover officer pull her gun from the back of her pants as she flew out of her seat, running toward the man. Just then the agitated citizen triumphantly yanked a large American flag out of his bag and demanded to know why people didn't know how to handle it properly. The officer tucked her weapon back into her pants, glanced at us, and walked out of the chambers.

12:30 A.M.

Finally, everyone has run out of speeches. I close the meeting, and in the parking lot I have one last chat with my exec. We debrief each other about the events of the evening. The verdict is that we accomplished much of what we wanted . . . or so we think, but neither one of us is thinking clearly anymore. I drive home with all the windows rolled down. By the time I get there, I'm wide awake again.

1:00 A.M.
I'm home. My spouse is asleep. I kiss her on the forehead, and, "wired," I go and try to grade a few more blue books.

TUESDAY

6:30 A.M.
I'm too tired to run this morning. Instead, I sit with a cup of coffee and read the paper's account of the day before. I'm still surprised, after all these years, that an entire day's worth of collective decision-making, based on months of prior work, is distilled into a few column inches. There is no flavor in these stories for the angst, the hard work, or the context of our decisions. I switch to the sports section.

7:30 A.M.
Back to the gentle womb of the university. I prepare for my first class. Finding extra time, I work on some research involving a book-length project with a colleague. The phone rings several times. I'm not answering.

10:00 A.M.
The subject in class today is the effect of nationalism on foreign policy. In the aftermath of the cold war and the end of the Soviet Union, we have a spirited discussion.

11:30 A.M.
Office hours start and students are waiting to see me. As I chat with each in turn, the ringing of the phone persistently intrudes on our conversations.

1:30 P.M.
Office hours are over and I check my phone messages. I return the call from my exec. Evidently, we can help expand the efforts of a local firm that has products needed in Eastern Europe. I agree to meet with the CEO "after work" tomorrow.

2:00 P.M.

I look over my notes for my next class. Fortunately, I prepared extensively before the start of the semester. Today's preparation is basically a review.

3:00 P.M.

The class topic focuses on the way in which the media translate candidates and campaigns to voters during presidential elections. Once more we are safely removed from local governance.

4:30 P.M.

I drive back to city hall. A group of Guatemalan mayors is visiting. I spend time with them describing what mayors do in the United States. Something must be lost in translation: Their eyes are glazed over.

5:15 P.M.

My spouse fixes us something to eat as soon as I get back home. We chat about our day, and as usual I find myself monopolizing the conversation.

6:00 P.M.

I do an hour-long interview on a radio station; I get to do it from home. The subject is spring training, and I'm trying to generate public support for the funding needed to attract a new baseball franchise. We take some calls to the station, and I discover that they are all from baseball fans supporting our efforts.

7:00 P.M.

Once off the phone, I spend the next three hours on university business. I work on a draft of a book chapter, then finish grading blue books. My spouse screens a number of calls, taking people's names and telling them I will call them back tomorrow.

10:00 P.M.

We go to bed early.

A year after I became mayor, I was taken out to lunch by a friend who had worked on several of my campaigns. Her purpose in getting together with me was to tell me that, since becoming mayor, I had become inaccessible to my friends. She wanted to let me know that I was no longer available to them the way that I had been before becoming mayor, and she wanted to know why I was deserting them. She told me that I was letting them down by not spending more time with them, and she felt that they were no longer "good enough" for me.

I tried to explain to her how little time there was in the day for a personal life. I don't think she believed me. We parted strangers.

6

Making Sausage

"Making laws is like making sausage. You'll like the taste once you're actually eating it, but not if you see how it's made."[23]

"We already have gender-neutral titles in politics. Crook, liar, thief, pinhead."[24]

City council chambers hold little physical resemblance to a scientist's laboratory—the trappings of power and authority dominate throughout the hall. The flags of nation, state, and city hang on the back wall. The seal of the city is prominently displayed on both the lectern and the dais facing the public. The dais is built of dark mahogany; the leather chairs behind it are oversized, dwarfing their more diminutive occupants.

In front of the dais stands a long wooden table surrounded by thirteen chairs. On top of the table are microphones, one for each member of the governing body and for the occasional bureaucrat who will be called on from time to time to share this space during meetings. Sandwiched between the table and the dais is another row of more modest chairs; these are for the council members' personal staff. In front of the table are a permanent stand and microphone; here is where those who wish to address the city council are asked to speak to the governing body. Hidden from public view is a set of three lights recessed into the stand and used during public hearings. Activated by the city clerk, they indicate when the speaker has exceeded allocated speaking time, and the flashing red light informs the speaker that it is time to conclude the remarks.

Stretching around the stand is a permanent wooden bar running the length of the room and barricading the government from the public area, where seats are fixed to the floor, capable of seating nearly 200 spectators and participants. At both ends of the bar are large, swiveling tripods on which are mounted television cameras focused on the city council. Hidden behind the dais in a closet-size room is a third camera, its lens fixed on the speaker's stand. All council meetings are televised live; each word and each act are permanently recorded, courtesy of the government channel and the city's cable operator.

The mayor sits in the largest chair on the dais. To the mayor's left sits the city clerk; the council members sit on the mayor's right. On the city clerk's left, separated by six feet of empty space, is another, smaller dais occupied by key municipal bureaucrats. The wall of the hallway leading out of the chambers is filled with official photos of the incumbent mayor and his thirty-eight predecessors. Only one is caught smiling; the rest seem to be suffering from various forms of stomach disorders.

The trappings of authority are not accompanied by visible means of security. There are no electronic metal detectors greeting visitors and citizens. There are no uniformed, armed police officers to scowl at angry constituents who come to voice their complaints to the governing body. Unless there has been some threat of disturbance, only one undercover police officer is in attendance and sits in the last row. There is one piece of additional security. After the assassination of San Francisco mayor George Moscone and county supervisor Harvey Milk by a colleague, the administration provided extra security by rebuilding the dais with reinforced steel under the mahogany cover. As a result, no crazed assassin can harm the bodies of elected officials in these chambers; their heads, however, remain vulnerable to attack.

This is the laboratory of local democracy. This is the place where decisions are made. The decisions create the experiments: Each law or policy passed in these chambers sets into motion a chain of events that impact on the life of the city and its residents.

This laboratory differs in many critical respects from the scientist's laboratory. The reservations and qualifications of scientific statements have no place in these chambers. According to the public officials here, the experiments undertaken are not a test of what will work but are the final statement of what needs to be done. Elected officials who would take the political risk of publicly recognizing that their actions constitute scientific guesswork—needing to be eventually amended or changed—would be immediately attacked for lacking direction, knowledge, or perspective of their community. They would be charged with betraying their campaign promises in coming to office: Those promises offered a direction that would work when implemented. In fact, first-time officeholders come to their positions with a sense of great certainty about their actions. It is only later that they discover that beliefs are not enough, and they come to discover how little hard knowledge is available about the consequences of their actions.

The experiments in the political laboratory are undertaken with oratorical certainty and with an expectation of total success. They will be defended in future campaigns as the best and only solutions that were available to pressing problems. Treating experiments as definitive solutions to problems is unavoidable in the democratic laboratory. Elected officials are not chosen to experiment but to lead and to solve problems without wasting resources and opportunities for citizens.

The local political laboratory differs from its scientific counterpart in another fundamental manner. The scientist records her observations and makes public the records of the experiment. In the municipal chambers, this process is made public in a dramatically different manner. Sunshine laws passed by states and municipalities require all deliberations and most of the steps in the experiment to be conducted in front of the public. In committee meetings, in "study sessions," and in formal meetings, all words and actions are recorded and followed by the media, interested citizens, and pressure groups. The municipal "scientist" is not evaluated on the basis of the results of the experiment but is scrutinized at every stage in the process, regardless of the eventual outcome. Citizens, special-interest groups, editorial writers, and television and radio commentators criticize, support, or denounce officials while the experiment is going on, and sometimes before the experiment has started. The scientist succeeds or fails by the eventual outcome of the experiment; in the democratic laboratory, the evaluation occurs even before a rezoning has had its impact or a road has been completed or a recycling program has been initiated.

Critical ingredients are sometimes spilled in the scientist's laboratory, and accidents and mistakes delay experiments. These miscalculations are not written up in the final, public presentation. All the warts, however, are evident in local government. Just as important, those in the minority on decisions often focus on potential mistakes to deflect the experiment, consciously jostling the experimenters to deter them from their tasks. Consequently, the people in the political laboratory spend a considerable amount of time not just on the experiment itself but on the actual presentation to the public of each step of the experiment. With the advent of television cameras recording each step in the process live, the municipal laboratory can become an elaborately orchestrated and scripted play superimposed on the experimental procedure.

This type of scrutiny is necessary and unavoidable if democratic governance is to be truly democratic. Sunshine laws and public exposure to decisions make life significantly more difficult at the local level, but they introduce a degree of accountability that is important to the functioning of democratic governance. Microscopic public attention to the process serves to highlight the involvement of special interests and unusual pressures on elected officials engaged in the making of public policy.

The net effect of watching and criticizing the "making of sausage" before tasting it should be, on the whole, a positive one from the standpoint of reducing the interference of special interests and of upgrading the performance of public officials by placing the entire process under constant scrutiny. As difficult as political life is under such circumstances, most municipal officials have been supportive of efforts to create more stringent sunshine laws and have pioneered the use of live television coverage of meetings.

Nevertheless, a major drawback to constant exposure at each stage in the process of governing is that the focus typically comes to rest on how the sausage is made and not on how it tastes. It is not unusual to see voters removing officials from office in response to controversy over the process of the experiment even though the results succeeded in addressing the problem.

The failure to focus on the outcome of the experiment has long-term impact both for the community and for those who occupy elected positions. Looking good in the process of making sausage is akin to waging a campaign for office—it requires good media skills; an ability to deliver short, concise analyses of problems; and a talent for projecting a positive personality on television. Unfortunately, these are not necessarily the skills of a good scientist or a good policy maker. While some who are good at policy making can develop the skills for looking good during the experimental process, the preoccupation with looking good at each stage of the experiment takes away precious time and resources from the nature of the experiment and its eventual success. Unless there is enough trust and empathy among citizens and the media to understand the nature of governance, few opportunities will exist for interested citizens to refocus eventually on the outcome of the experiment. And as long as elected officials find it impossible to refocus public attention from sausage making to sausage tasting, they will be caught in a vicious circle in which looking good during the process becomes an all-consuming aspect of governance.

The need to look good during the making of public policies is not unique to the municipal level. Politicians in state and federal politics suffer from the same disease. At the local level, however, there are unique aspects to the problem. First, the scrutiny is greater. Municipal officials get more ink and airtime than their national counterparts and must look good more often and more consistently. While Congress or the state legislature may, as institutions, receive similar scrutiny, seldom is this true for the specific behavior of most members of those institutions. Second, greater scrutiny is accompanied by greater and more immediate feedback. How you looked at Monday's meeting is immediately translated that evening on television and radio, and the next morning on the front page and in the editorial section of the newspaper. Finally, local officials differ from their state and national counterparts in the fact that they are not "professionals" at looking good. As we saw in Chapter 3, most local officials are amateur politicians, less skilled in the craft of looking good than are their professional counterparts. Ironically, the lack of professional status often leads to their working harder at policy—the principal motivation in running for office—to compensate for their shortcomings in looking good during the process.

THE RANGE OF EXPERIMENTS

Complex experiments occur in the scientist's laboratory, with the scientist giving her undivided attention to a specific experiment. This represents another fundamental difference in the local democratic laboratory. At the council table, the list of experiments progressing simultaneously is contained in the dreaded "agenda book" chronicling the items to be acted upon at each meeting. Here is a partial list of one city council's experiments addressed at a meeting during the first week of August, in the order in which they were discussed:

- Discussion to release city lands from public to private use.
- Discussion to create a partnership to develop more public facilities for children downtown.
- Discussion to limit the scope and functions of youth night clubs in the city.
- Discussion to identify citizens for voluntary boards and commissions advising elected officials and city staff.
- Discussion to assist financially, and to promote the meeting of, western governors in the city.
- Discussion on three separate requests to rezone property for future development.
- Discussion to change the city's scenic corridor law to allow for future development.
- Discussion of appeal from a previous staff decision denying a type of land use downtown.
- Discussion of legal strategies to represent the city on water legislation before the state and federal governments.
- Discussion of a new compensation plan for city employees.
- Discussion of a new ordinance providing job protection to city employees for "whistle-blowing" activities.
- Discussion of a final development plan for the east side of the community.
- Discussion on the naming of city streets.
- Discussion of three zoning ordinances to be adopted.
- Discussion of election procedures for upcoming local offices.
- Discussion of a cooperative program with state law enforcement agencies for metropolitan drug enforcement.
- Discussion of a cooperative program with state commerce officials for use of the state housing trust fund.
- Discussion of three separate projects to create neighborhood improvement districts.
- Discussion of a cooperative program with the state's attorney general's office to implement a victim's rights assistance program.
- Discussion of a joint venture with the state's board of regents to pursue a project to demonstrate water-conservation methods.

- Discussion of a demonstration project to divert arterial traffic from neighborhoods.
- Discussion of a potential agreement with the telephone company for use of city property.
- Discussion of sale of city properties to other jurisdictions.
- Discussion of a multijurisdictional approach to fighting metropolitan drug trafficking.
- Discussion of a cooperative program with other local jurisdictions for public transportation services.
- Discussion of metropolitan para-transit services for citizens with disabilities.
- Discussion of agreements with county facilities for jail services.
- Discussion of strategies for investing city employees' retirement funds.
- Discussion of cooperation strategies with the state department of transportation for maintenance of major arterial streets.
- Discussion of attorney services for indigent citizens appearing in the city's courts.
- Discussion of a special election to amend the charter of the city, calling for nonpartisan and ward-based elections.
- Discussion of a demonstration project for low-income housing and application of funding with the federal government.
- Discussion on creating appropriate polling places and designating elections boards for the upcoming primary elections.
- Discussion of contract services for expanding recreational facilities on the south side of the community.
- Discussion on the issuance of seventeen separate liquor licenses throughout the community.
- Discussion on issuing a contract to investigate and mitigate potential contamination to the city's aquifer.
- Discussion on attempts to stabilize inner-city neighborhoods through cooperative strategies with the school districts on elementary school development.
- Discussion of food programs for the homeless downtown.
- Discussion on plans to expand recreational programs for juveniles and the use of golf surcharges for financing these programs.
- Discussion of strategies for increasing security at city facilities.
- Discussion of requests from the Hispanic community to provide city support for events celebrating the community's heritage.

- Discussion of request for funds from the Native American community to assist with housing development.
- Discussion of request for funds from the Hispanic chamber of commerce to assist with activities related to the North American Free Trade Agreement (NAFTA).
- Discussion of two appeals regarding the city's policy on time constraints involving rezoning laws.
- Discussion on several demonstration projects for the feasibility of recharging Central Arizona Project (CAP) water.
- Discussion of the scope and costs of lobbying representation in Washington, D.C.
- Discussion in executive session of two legal cases involving the city, and presently being adjudicated in court.
- Discussion on the quality of water being diverted to the community from the CAP.
- Discussion of new city policy regarding the disposition of garbage.
- Discussion regarding negotiations with a major employer in the city about potential contamination of groundwater.

On this particular Monday, in a meeting that started around 1:30 P.M. and would last late into the evening hours, each member of the city council was asked to make a public decision and to look good on ninety-eight separate items. Only thirteen of the items represented issues brought to the table by members of the governing body. Nearly 90 percent of the issues discussed were there at the request of the city bureaucracy, individual citizens, special-interest groups, or other governments. In the large majority of cases, the initiatives of the policy makers were crowded off the agenda by other matters, and these politicians were required to act reasonably on issues often outside their province of major concern, interest, and knowledge. In this particular laboratory, the experimenters were juggling experiments often not of their own making, and they juggled a dangerously high volume of experiments.

Not all items are equally important to everyone in the community, and some will have far-reaching effects while others will impact only a handful of residents. Yet nearly all are potentially explosive and must be treated with care. Particularly if the entire laboratory is being evaluated in large part by how members conduct themselves inside the laboratory, great care must be taken even with minor issues (these are called "consent agenda" items, signifying agreement that they are minor and need no discussion, but they can be, and often are, pulled out for discussion anyway). Mistakes on issues that may affect only a handful of people but that are likely to explode on television or in the newspapers as that handful of citizens denounce the process and the participants will further erode the credibility of the process for other experiments.

TACKLING NEW EXPERIMENTS

The certainty with which these experiments are undertaken at the local level betrays a new phenomenon occurring throughout most municipal settings: Most of the policy areas being tackled are relatively new, and local policy makers are being thrust into experiments with which they have had little previous experience. Historically, cities had to deal with a relatively finite set of problems and with relatively stable resources available for their experiments. Land-use patterns; garbage collection; emergency and public services such as police, fire, and paramedics; and the construction of infrastructure occupied the public policy agenda in most locales. Municipal public policies historically focused on conflicts over resources for basic services and the extent to which the tax base should be enhanced to address activities beyond basic services (such as recreation or assistance for the arts). These issues were by no means simple, but there was a historical record guiding the experimenters even if they were not experts.

Two major changes over the past two decades have fundamentally altered the nature of these experiments. First, the role of the federal government with respect to urban areas greatly diminished at a time of increasing urban problems, leaving states and primarily municipalities to deal with issues with which they had little previous experience. The Reagan administration's new federalism, in particular, shifted a broad range of domestic problems to municipalities without providing any accompanying resources or expertise to address those problems.

Although the Reagan administration was unequivocal and persistent in its new federalism policy, its actions served only to accelerate a second trend toward more local responsibility in most modern, Western democracies. Suddenly, the nature of the experiments changed in the local laboratory. Local officials, who knew a great deal about municipal traffic but not as much about energy issues, were asked to experiment with alternative-fuel options and air-pollution mitigation. Officials who knew how to pick up the garbage and put it in landfills were now focusing on recycling strategies and the problem of combating environmental degradation caused by landfills. Council members whose knowledge of television was limited to watching it were now asked to develop long-term telecommunications scenarios for their cities and to do battle with the cable industry, the phone companies, and federal regulators. Mayors, whose knowledge of economic policy was limited to boosting the value of their cities to prospective businesses, were now forced to engage in long-term economic planning, testing theories of the market and launching overseas initiatives in search of both investment and employment opportunities. With the end of the cold war and the growing economic impact of reductions in defense contracts and closures of military bases, municipalities even tried to influence national defense and foreign policies and flirted with their own economic conversion programs.

The new federalism meant as well that many social welfare functions traditionally addressed at the federal and state levels would crash down on the urban areas. As poverty increased and low-wage jobs supplemented the loss of better-paying employment, cities were faced increasingly with the option of denouncing Washington or engaging in further experimentation. The provision of low-income housing, long a province of the federal government, shrank at a time when the need was rising. Federal support for transit subsidies was fading. Federal retraining and employment programs were slashed, often by as much as 60 percent, while a shrinking safety net produced increased misery. Such misery in the urban areas was manifested in an upsurge of homelessness, increased crime, and an explosive environment in the public school systems, especially in low-income neighborhoods. To the extent that these problems coincided with ethnic and racial divisions, they further exacerbated the quality of life in the nation's cities.

Ironically, as municipalities were forced to take on greater responsibilities, their resources were shrinking. Federal support did not accompany the shift in responsibility to the local level. Even in those few states where sympathetic governors and legislators tried to assist municipalities, officials quickly found that state coffers were drying up as the national economy plunged into recession. Local jurisdictions started raising taxes, but even the most innovative soon found that they lacked the financial resources to adequately address the range of new problems they were tackling. By the start of the 1990s, urban officials were confronted with new wide-ranging and complex problems at a time of deteriorating economic conditions and diminished resources.

THE PEOPLE IN THE LAB COATS

Juggling many complex experiments is not an easy task. The example of the council meeting illustrated above requires expertise in no fewer than twenty-three different public policy areas.[25] This problem of "expertise" is resolved in state and federal legislatures by their large size and consequent ability to specialize through committees. This answer is seldom available at the local level. Local politicians exist in governing bodies that are relatively small. In a typical city of a half-million people, the city council may consist of only seven people. Even in New York City, the largest city in the United States, the governing body consists of about fifty elected officials to represent the needs of 9 million constituents. In only a handful of the nation's largest cities—including Chicago, New York, Indianapolis, Nashville, and St. Louis—do city councils enjoy the "luxury" of having more than twenty elected officials on the governing body, allowing for some semblance of specialization, expertise, and focused attention to policy areas. In Los Angeles, the nation's second largest city, fifteen council members fashion public policy. A substantial number of states with less than half the population of Los Angeles have six to ten times as many legislators as Los Angeles has council members. The paucity of municipal officials makes specialization difficult, if not impossible. Unlike members of Congress who specialize in certain aspects of policy, council members don't have the luxury of taking policy cues from one another in policy areas where they may lack expertise. In effect, they must specialize in nearly every aspect of public policy.

Given their limited numbers, neither can local officials deflect public scrutiny from their individual actions on policy decisions. Each member of a small governing body is all too visible and will be held accountable on each issue. None will have the luxury of watching a committee chair take public responsibility for a particular course of action.

City officials must operate as well in a context of limited staffing

assistance with their work. They seldom have the equivalent of a legislative research service or office staff to provide information and analysis
relatively free from or untainted by the agendas of others in the political
arena. In the U.S. House of Representatives, for example, members
avail themselves of an average of seventeen staff people per office, ex-
cluding the staff serving on over 300 committees and in the four research agencies under the legislative branch. In many large cities, where
a council member may represent more people than a member of Congress, the typical council office may consist of no more than a secretary
and, if fortunate, one or two aides (one of whom is working exclusively
on constituent concerns).

Apart from their own staff, municipal leaders can make use of the
expertise in the city's administrative structure. Within any city bureaucracy there are many departments containing a wealth of expertise.
The police department can tell you how to fight crime. The planning
department can provide information on the effects of a rezoning. Most
city managers have their own budget and research departments to provide additional analysis. At its best, however, this is filtered and tainted
information. It comes from and is filtered through administrative lenses,
seeing problems either from the standpoint of a particular department
or from the vantage point of administering policies. Information that
may cast a negative light on previous administrative performance, or
information that would lead to policies making life more difficult for
those providing the information, is not likely to be available to the
policy maker. This is why legislators in Congress cannot afford to rely
on the president for information and must develop their own sources of
knowledge. Otherwise, they would be totally dependent on and become captives of the federal bureaucracy and would be unable to oversee what the bureaucracy does.

Unfortunately, the issue of who has control over information is a
great and ongoing concern in the laboratory of municipal government.
If the experimenters lack sufficient information to gauge the impact of
their experiments, experiments will be conducted blindly. Worse still,
experimenters cannot proceed in a meaningful way if they don't have
sufficient data to understand the appropriate mix of ingredients needed
for the experiment.

Consider one typical example of this information problem. One
city's elected officials decided to tackle the problem of traffic congestion

on their streets. The transportation department recommended construction of a new freeway around the city. The impact of the freeway construction was considerable, costing well over $600 million, and the process of construction would have destroyed scores of neighborhoods and businesses in its path. The city council wanted an alternative: building bantam interchanges on several north-south and east-west arterial streets through which traffic would pass under the intersections, avoiding backups and air pollution from too many cars idling at traffic lights. The bantam interchanges, compact in design, would be superimposed on existing street patterns, minimizing harm to existing neighborhoods and businesses, and would be constructed at a fraction of the cost of a new freeway.

The city's transportation department was opposed to the council's idea. Building freeways is what engineers and traffic experts do well, and the bantam concept was tricky. Furthermore, from a strictly transportation perspective, freeways were judged to be more efficient for channeling the flow of vehicular traffic. Finally, transportation people are not in the business of saving neighborhoods or designing ways of saving money on transportation projects for nontransportation problems. The transportation department opposed the council's policy preference (politely) but offered to provide whatever information was needed to evaluate the council's preferred alternative.

The city council had no engineers or traffic experts among its ranks, forcing it to rely on the bureaucracy for the needed information. The transportation department developed data showing that each interchange would require the acquisition of substantial amounts of right-of-way, leading to major dislocations of both businesses and neighborhoods. Finally, the construction schedule showed severe disruption to existing transportation throughout the community for years while the bantams were being constructed.

The city council, suspecting tainted information, argued with its own "experts" and questioned whether the designed bantams, which were much larger than anticipated and the reason for all the bad news, were unnecessarily large. The transportation department's legal experts—also in the bureaucracy and beyond the control of elected officials—then told the council that the designed size constituted the minimal configuration needed to meet minimum federal safety standards. Thus, the council was placed in a legally untenable position. The politicians could decide to build interchanges that did not meet federal safety rules, but if accidents occurred, the city would be liable for millions of dollars in damages once the policy makers had been advised that they were in potential violation of federal guidelines. The council members reluctantly backed down.

With a sizable independent staff providing information untainted by bureaucratic interests, the outcome could have been very different. The members of the governing body did not know, and it was not in the interest of the transportation department to tell them, that the federal rules for interchanges were developed in the 1950s for the design of the interstate system, which was built in part to accommodate the transportation of intercontinental ballistic missiles. The city council's position was essentially correct, although it did not have the information to show that it was correct. Smaller bantams could have been built at low cost, without dislocation, and with relatively minor disruption in existing service, and the city would not have had legal liability as long as it prohibited the transportation of intercontinental ballistic missiles across its main arterial streets.

In the absence of empathy toward the conditions operating in the laboratory, it is easy to blame either the bureaucracy or the policy makers for failing to resolve this particular city's transportation problems in a cost-effective manner. The transportation department was correct in urging an approach that from the standpoint of engineers (focusing strictly on traffic flows) was the best long-term solution. It was the responsibility of the governing body to weigh this alternative against other problems and other objectives (such as neighborhood and business preservation). The governing body was equally correct in searching for a solution that would maximize both the goals of smoother traffic and savings to the treasury. It was also correct in not proceeding with the experiment when the available information indicated that the experiment would fail. Unfortunately, in this particular city the problem is still not being addressed. The city doesn't have the revenue to build the freeway option, and given the controversy over bantams, public support for this alternative has dissipated. Meanwhile, traffic congestion is worse than ever.

Ironically, the issue was critically affected by a forgotten proposal by the city council six years before the bantam discussion. At that time the council brought before the voters an initiative to create a research service under the jurisdiction of the city council. Had the initiative passed, the additional staffing available to the council could have provided the information to go ahead with the experiment and, through it, to have a very positive effect on both traffic congestion and air pollution. However, the initiative failed before the voters. Opponents argued that the city bureaucracy was large enough, that additional staffing would waste taxpayer dollars, and that elected officials should know enough about problems, and if they didn't people should elect better-quality officials. The opposition was led by a group of businesspeople who had good working relationships with the existing bureaucracy and was able to influence it better than it could members of the city council. In the absence of empathy toward local officials and the process of governance, the opposition was heard more clearly than the proponents and the initiative went down to defeat. In this particular city today, the politicians are routinely blamed for the "outrageous gridlock" and the air pollution caused by cars idling at intersections. Much of the criticism comes from the same businesspeople who opposed the council staffing initiative years earlier.

It is plausible that even without additional staffing the city council could have discovered the needed information to conduct the bantam experiment had the members of the governing body focused exclusively on this issue. Such single-minded experimentation, however, is unrealistic to expect in the modern urban municipality. The bantam issue played out in the context of dozens of simultaneous experiments, with most of them encountering the same problems of limited access to quality information.

THE STRUCTURE OF THE LABORATORY

Historically, experimentation has occurred not only with public policies but with the structure of the laboratory as well. From a structural standpoint, urban governments in America have experimented with a variety of political laboratories. One type—the strong-mayor form—reflects the government structure at the federal level: multiple laboratories, with strict separation of powers between them. In this structure, the legislative body and the mayor are elected separately, with the council held accountable for policy decisions and the mayor held accountable for the administration of the city. A separate, independent judiciary exists (elected or appointed, depending on local custom) to enforce and interpret local laws. In this structure, council members may oversee, but they cannot be involved in, the daily administration of the city. Likewise, the mayor may create policy initiatives but is dependent on the council for their passage and their funding. New York City is typical of this type of laboratory.

A second structural arrangement blurs the boundaries between administrative and legislative laboratories. Often called a council-manager form of government, it has an elected body that includes both mayor and council members, making policy decisions together. The mayor, who formally speaks for the city, is primarily a legislator. The administration of the city is the responsibility of a city manager (appointed by the city council), who serves at the pleasure of the council. All the administrative units of the city report to the city manager and are directed by the manager. The manager may make policy recommendations, but his primary responsibility rests with the administration of the city and the implementation of policies. Unlike the mayor-council structure, the council-manager type of government removes administrative authority from the direct control of the voters. Phoenix represents one example of this form of government.

A third arrangement—the municipal cabinet form—blurs further the distinction between administrative and policy laboratories. In this structure, the mayor and council are elected by the voters. The mayor may initiate policies and is primarily responsible for the administration of the city. Council members, however, are given department "portfolios" and become the heads of one or more administrative departments. This arrangement is similar to the British parliamentary model of cabinet officers coming from the legislative ranks and is practiced in the city of Portland, Oregon.

These three types of arrangement for the local political laboratory provide important options and trade-offs for experimentation with public policy. In the council-manager laboratory, elected officials are isolated from the daily administrative affairs of the city. They can spend most of their deliberations on legislative tasks. They are, however, more insulated than in the other laboratories from the daily impact of their decisions, and they are able to exercise less impact on how their legislative mandates are being carried out. In addition, they are held responsible for administrative activities over which they have little control, short of firing the city manager. While firing the manager seems like a formidable weapon, it is a crude one and cannot be used often.

The strong-mayor system of governance addresses directly the issue of administrative accountability: The mayor is responsible to the public for all bureaucratic activities in the city. The mandate for the mayor comes from the public and separately from the city council, and as a result, the conflicts over the direction of experiments are likely to escalate rapidly in this type of laboratory. Such conflicts are not unhealthy in a democracy: They provide alternative perspectives on ongoing experiments. Such conflicts, however, are healthy only as long as the public understands the reasons behind the conflicts. When empathy and trust are in decline, conflicts between mayors and councils are often viewed by the public as counterproductive and as acts of "political bickering."

The integration of administrative and legislative functions in cities such as Portland seems most alien to what we consider to be the separation of powers in American politics. Certainly both its virtues and its drawbacks are clear. On the one hand, this system allows legislators to fully implement their decisions in a manner consistent with their intent, allowing for a fuller opportunity to truly experiment with a given policy. There is no need to filter decisions through complex bureaucracies or to worry about clashing with department heads who may hold agendas different from those of the legislators. On the other hand, this political laboratory reduces the opportunity to check legislative reality against administrative plausibility. The brakes placed on legislative mandates by the difficulties uncovered in implementing policy decisions become weaker in this system. Furthermore, by forcing legislators to be both administrators and policy makers, the system requires the electorate to choose very wisely among those running for office and demands a level of competence from candidates above and beyond their ability to represent the public. It also means that elected officials must be full-time, well-paid professionals.

Two other structural considerations may impact on these different types of laboratories. One concerns the fragmentation or integration of different types of local political units. Some urban areas, for example, have ongoing experiments with the consolidation of city and county governments (for example, Indianapolis and Nashville). Geographically distinct entities are merged, creating a regional executive and a regional council to integrate policies and resources. While these efforts have typically been sold to citizens as methods by which duplication of administrative functions is reduced and taxes are utilized more efficiently, the evidence for these impacts is quite limited. Structural changes of this type, however, have reduced the financial problems associated with urban flight and the fragmentation of public policies across large urban areas.

While the integration of structures has occurred in some areas, these trends have coexisted with a tendency to fragment municipal government further and to increase the number of laboratories through which public policy experimentation is occurring. Most urban areas with competing municipal governments have developed councils of governments (COGs) where all jurisdictions in a metropolitan area sit together in response to federal and state mandates. At the same time, there has been a proliferation of functional bodies charged with raising taxes, making policy, and administering one specific area of policy. People serving on such bodies are sometimes appointed, but more often they are elected to office in nonpartisan elections. Water districts, sanitation districts, library districts, school boards, and transportation districts are typical of these structures throughout the nation's urban areas.

Typically, these functional laboratories have been developed to insulate a certain area or activity from other policy decisions by trying to take the policy area out of the traditional political process. Unfortunately, such well-meaning reforms can backfire on their architects. A recent example occurred in Los Angeles, where the community created a separate board to oversee the activities of its police chief. The "reform" was undertaken to take law enforcement oversight out of the political process. Yet in doing so, this structural change made it impossible for those who are held accountable to the public—the mayor and council—to control the activities of their own police chief, and they could not fire the person they appointed to run the police department. When police chief Daryl Gates was accused of failing to respond quickly to emergencies during the Los Angeles riots and failing to discipline officers who were videotaped using excessive force on a citizen, the governing body found that it could not fire him. When Gates finally left the department, he did so in his own time and on his own terms despite the desire of both the governing body and the citizens of Los Angeles to get rid of him.

A second structural consideration concerns the relationship between public employees, their managers, and the governing body. In the transportation example given above, city employees withheld vital information from the governing body. Why weren't they disciplined? Why didn't the city hire transportation experts who might subordinate their interests or perspectives to those of the governing body? The answers are simple. They served in a municipal structure governed by civil service rules and regulations. All 300 employees of the transportation department, including the department head, were in the civil service, had been employed by the city before the election of the governing body, and would continue to work for the city well after the mayor and council members left office. Even if the city council wanted to replace the leadership of the transportation department with people who shared its policy orientations toward air pollution or neighborhood preservation, civil service rules would have prohibited the changes. These rules were enacted as a series of reforms to protect the public from politicians who could be tempted to use the city's payroll to reward their supporters. The practical results, however, have been that politicians in the laboratory are forced to rely on information for their experiments from people whose interests and perspectives do not necessarily coincide with those trying to design the experiments.

These structural differences are not trivial. They have a critical impact on what can be accomplished in the laboratory and the manner in which experiments will be conducted. The lack of understanding about these differences by the media and citizens leads to false expectations and unfair evaluations of what elected officials can do in office. Elected officials cannot be expected to rein in the bureaucracy if they have no legal control over it. Council members of a city may be blamed for failing to control air pollution and transportation gridlock, but when governments are fragmented in a metropolitan area, these officials will lack the authority to implement measures to address regional problems. When elected officials lack access to vital information needed to do a good job, they may blame the structure of the laboratory, but whether or not they are correct, the public will blame the politicians, not the structural problems that may have caused these failures.

A laboratory that is structurally deficient for developing good public policy breeds further distrust of elected officials and the political system.

Politicians who fail to meet the expectations of the public because they are constrained by the weaknesses in the political laboratory can and will be replaced, but unless the laboratory itself is appropriate for the local circumstances, their successors will fail as well, leading to the self-fulfilling prophecy that politics and politicians will be incompetent. Structurally deficient laboratories need to be rebuilt, but in the absence of empathy and a disappearance of trust in the governors, the pleas of officeholders to change the structure of the laboratory will fall on deaf ears.

EXPERIMENTING WITH PUBLIC POLICIES

"You are doing a lousy job. If you want to know who I am, I'm not going to give you my name. You are not doing the job you think you're supposed to be doing. You're not doing nothing. Why haven't you done anything for us? That's all I have to say."[26]

The work in the political laboratory is no less challenging and perhaps far more difficult than the work in the scientific laboratory. Extensive experimentation occurs in both because there is no other fruitful way to knowledge and the consequent resolution of problems. Activities in both types of laboratories are driven by theoretical frameworks that provide the tools needed to understand how the world works, and the experiments in the laboratories are designed to apply working theories to specific problems. In the scientific laboratory, experimenting with potential solutions to problems allows scientists to reassess their understanding of physical life, and by so doing to help refine their tools for future experiments and problem solving.

In the political laboratory, however, the tools available for solving problems are far more blunt than in the scientist's laboratory. No less than three major problems stand in the way of the policy maker's success. First is the information gap. The information available to those who make public policy is far less systematic and less available than for the scientist. The scientist relies on extensive evidence systematically collected both in the past and currently in numerous laboratories within the scientific community. The evidence is available in assorted journals, books, and data banks. In the political laboratory, there is scant equivalence in data collection. While extensive research services are available at the federal level, the quality and quantity of systematic and historically accurate information on problems dramatically decrease at the state and local levels despite heroic efforts to share information by organizations of administrators and elected officials. Yet without significant and systematic information about the nature of the problem being addressed, finding satisfactory solutions is a daunting task.

A second problem revolves around the lack of comprehensive understanding. Policy makers lack the explanatory frameworks available to scientists with which to pursue their public policy decisions. Scientific theories, which provide a road map for solving problems, have a long history of evolution, validation, and constant testing against rigorous scientific standards. In the world of science, such theories ultimately may prove to be wrong or useless, and then they will be discredited, as will those scientists who insist on using them. Just as likely, scientific theories often represent the best and most useful cumulative analytical approaches available in the scientific community. There is no such counterpart for public policy knowledge in the political laboratory. Policy makers may possess some vague ideological frameworks with which to approach problems, but clearly a liberal or conservative approach of the type utilized by policy makers in America's political laboratories is far from the rigor of scientific theory.

Furthermore, political explanations of public policy, unlike many scientific theories, seem to have a life of their own even when they fail to achieve desired results. For example, the trickle-down economics of tax reductions in the 1980s looks suspiciously like the forerunner of the Contract with America espoused by a new Republican congressional majority in 1995. One leading contender for the presidential nomination on the Republican side in 1996 had even taken to proclaiming he was simply a foot soldier for trickle-down economics. Yet this political approach in the 1980s led to greater income inequalities for most Americans and skyrocketing federal budget deficits—policy objectives that were to be avoided in the 1990s.

Political theories of social life may be held by elected officials and applied to the problems of society because the policy makers feel an affinity toward a particular ideology or find it politically expedient to believe in it. Irrespective of available evidence, and perhaps because the systematic evidence is too sketchy to truly test the value of a particular approach, even vague theories and ideological guidelines are used in the political laboratory to provide some sense of direction for public policies.

There are severe consequences to not having an equivalent of rigorous scientific theories in the political laboratory. One consequence is that, in the absence of an explanatory framework that is being constantly improved and made more efficient, the answers that policy makers generate for pressing societal problems will not work as efficiently as they and the public would hope. This means that great care must be taken with public policies. Policy decisions need to be constantly scrutinized for their impact on the public, and those who work in the political laboratory must be flexible enough to change policies to adjust to circumstances that they could not have anticipated without a sharper understanding of societal dynamics. Here lies a difficult dilemma for the political laboratory: Experimentation becomes even more important for the formulation of public policies than in the pursuit of scientific knowledge, but, ironically, experimentation is even more hazardous and difficult without the theoretical knowledge and empirical data available to scientists in their laboratories. Unfortunately, in the absence of trust and empathy toward those who make decisions, likely "failures" in the political laboratory will be far less tolerated in the public sphere than in the scientific laboratory, and the entire system may be jeopardized as citizens lose patience with their governors.

A third problem unique to the political laboratory is lack of ability to control the variables, and it revolves around the type of evidence available with which to judge the success of experiments. Trying to determine how successful public policies are is made more difficult by the interdependence inherent in all complex social problems. Scientific problems may be no less complex than sociopolitical ones, but in the scientist's laboratory specific problems can be isolated. For example, the effects of a particular virus can be examined regardless of the biological mechanism that will ultimately be its host, and scientists can examine the effects that such a virus will have under a variety of circumstances. This is not the case with social problems. Most societal problems and issues are interdependent, and even a wise answer may fail because other circumstances could not be controlled. Individuals and entire communities of citizens cannot be treated as guinea pigs and subjected to experiments whereby one and then another social process is altered to determine the independent effects of each process on individuals and society. Yet without such controls it is impossible to tell if the solution to a particular problem has failed or if the solution would have been successful had other problems not intruded. This is not a trivial distinction. If the approach to the problem would have worked, everything else being equal, this conclusion would allow policy makers to move on to address other problems that may have interfered with the proposed solution. Conversely, if the initial approach was unworkable, then new solutions must be found. If, however, policy makers lack the information to distinguish between these two outcomes, then it becomes virtually impossible to decide whether to continue with one approach or to shift to another. In this manner, the absence of "controls" in the political laboratory creates great difficulties for policy makers when the problems on which they work don't seem to respond to the solutions they have devised.

Even when a policy approach has been successful in addressing a problem, it is difficult to ascertain success. On rare occasions, there are indicators that a solution has worked can be found in statistics, such as declining inflation or reduced unemployment rates. But these are relatively rare instances of "hard data" accompanying specific problems. Much more likely, evidence is not available to indicate that a problem is being addressed successfully, particularly when objective indicators may not address the social problem being perceived by the public. It is possible, for example, that efforts at addressing the problem of crime are working, but what do declining crime statistics mean when people actually feel that crime is increasing and fear for their security?

Even when objective indicators of societal conditions could reflect reality, often they are not available. For example, the core of the public policy debate and experimentation about welfare and economic policies in general has to do with how much true employment opportunity exists for those Americans who are struggling to make ends meet. It is widely assumed that opportunities to work and to get ahead exist for both those on welfare (thus, the debate turns on welfare dependence) and those in low-paying jobs. Yet neither the government nor academia has produced an objective measure of economic opportunity regardless of the importance that such an indicator would have for the political laboratory and for the political currents that swirl around this important issue. In fact, some evidence indicates that there is far less opportunity available in the workforce than needed by unemployed citizens and underpaid workers. As many as 16 million well-paid jobs may be needed in the national economy to accommodate people who are working but who cannot generate enough income to raise themselves above the poverty level in America. Knowing this simple fact would dramatically alter approaches to "workfare" and poverty. Without such measures, however, public policy debates and policy experimentation are hopelessly mired in rhetoric, without much hope of creating policies that will have a substantial effect on the lives of citizens seeking to realize the American dream.[27]

Instead of relying on hard evidence to substantiate success, policy makers are often forced to consider one of two other measures. One is the grumblemeter: a measure based on public feedback. If people grumble less about a certain problem, it is assumed that the option deployed by government is working. Of course, it is just as likely that people have grown weary of protest and comment, or that other problems have become temporarily more salient for them.

The second measure is success or failure at the ballot box: Elections resulting in the defeat or retention of incumbents are supposed to be the ultimate indication of whether the most salient problems are being addressed successfully. Unfortunately, this is a very blunt measure. It is hard to gauge which problems people are responding to when voting or whether the power of incumbency is so strong that it dulls the ability of challengers to contest for office in a meaningful way.

Even when it is perceived that people vote to change the status quo, it is difficult to determine what the outcome really means. Consider the elections of 1994. For the first time in forty years, control of both houses of Congress went to Republicans, signifying a stunning defeat for Democrats and the status quo. The election was interpreted in this manner by commentators and Republican policy makers alike. Republicans, especially, were citing the results as a repudiation of failed Democratic initiatives on social policies. Yet how valid is this interpretation? Did the 1994 elections provide evidence that the public had rejected activist national programs in favor of a smaller federal role in the lives of citizens? These were the allegations made by the "victors" and by substantial numbers of losers as well.

The problem of using election outcomes to measure the effectiveness of public policies is illustrated well by the elections of 1994. When all the votes are counted nationally, we discover that virtually half of the voters voted for each of the two political parties, while over 60 percent of eligible voters failed to express their preferences. Rather than a resounding defeat for existing policies, nearly one-half of all citizens who bothered to vote expressed support for Democratic candidates. The Democrats who lost their seats came overwhelmingly from congressional districts where they had won in very close elections only two years earlier. Yet with a lower Democratic turnout in 1994, a massive surge of Republican spending near the end of the elections, and a swing of 10 percent of independents from the Democratic to the Republican column, enough of these incumbents were defeated to change the composition of both houses of Congress. There is substantial evidence as well from public opinion polls to indicate that the crucial election issue revolved around virtually none of the points trumpeted by winners and losers. Instead, and just as in 1992, the outcome of the election seems to have revolved around the continuing loss of wages by both middle- and lower-income Americans, indicating that "It's [still] the economy, stupid."[28] If indeed this was the case, then it should have come as no surprise to the new Republican majority in Congress—interpreting the 1994 elections as a mandate for the Contract with America and implementing that mandate—that by 1995 the public was indicating in opinion polls a preference for Democrats over the governing Republican majority.

Did the Democrats lose Congress because the voters rejected their approach to the laboratory in favor of a conservative agenda (rejecting both the size of the laboratory and the range of public policy experiments being conducted), or were people indicating instead continuing unhappiness over their own economic well-being (showing dissatisfaction primarily with only those public policies that were failing to have a favorable effect on people's paychecks)? At one level, it doesn't matter. New people and a new party leadership were placed in the laboratory. But knowing which version of these "data" is valid is crucial if we believe that elections can be used to assess whether ongoing experiments are working. Unfortunately, it is virtually impossible to ascertain from these electoral outcomes whether specific policies are or are not working by means similar to the tests conducted in the scientific laboratory.

Each of these three problems—the information gap, the absence of comprehensive understanding, and the absence of control—poses substantial difficulties in the political laboratory. They are by no means unsolvable, but they make the lives of policy makers extremely difficult. Furthermore, these difficulties stand in sharp contrast to the rhetoric of many political critics who espouse "obvious" and simplistic solutions to societal problems and of other critics who believe that the reasons why governors fail to resolve problems have to do with an absence of caring, or incompetence, or worse.

POLICY MAKING AT THE LOCAL LEVEL

The problems involved with working in the political laboratory exist at all levels of government. At the local level, however, these problems impact differently than at other levels. The urban laboratory is considered to be a place where the complexity of social life is great, but it does not have to accommodate the diversity of interests that exist around the nation. Governing Phoenix, Detroit, Los Angeles, or Chicago requires tackling great complexity but not as much as trying to find one answer that will work equally well for the problems of all of these cities simultaneously (one of the central problems in trying to govern from Washington). No wonder, then, that so much experimentation can and does take place at the state and municipal levels. In the urban laboratory, it is still impossible to control for the whole range of issues that can destroy an experiment, but the number of issues that could potentially interfere with the experiment is smaller and more visible than at the national level.

While the problem of controlling the experiment is less onerous at the local level, the other two problems—the information gap and lack of comprehensive understanding—are perhaps more difficult to tackle. Systematic historical information about problems and solutions that have been tried before is more difficult to find for local policy makers. Municipalities lack the capability to assemble, integrate, and disseminate such information. As a result, experimenters in the municipal laboratory work under conditions of greater ignorance than do their national counterparts. One of the major reasons, however, for municipal membership in the International City Managers Association, the National League of Cities, and the U.S. Conference of Mayors is that these associations work very hard to amass information on what cities are and are not doing correctly, and they share this information with

their members. Without them, cities would labor in far greater ignorance. And because of their participation, individual elected officials
often find ways to address problems that they might not have contem-
plated otherwise.

The problem of having a good theoretical base for conducting the
experiment is shared at all political levels, but it is compounded at
the local level. In many municipalities, elections and the recruitment
of people into the laboratory occur in a legally nonpartisan environment. Mayors and council members in many cities do not run as Democrats or Republicans and are expected to govern without favoring
their respective parties or the orientations of their parties on public
policy. As a mayor of a midwestern city would often point out, "There
is no such thing as Democratic or Republican garbage. There is only
garbage, and the issue of municipal governance is whether it gets removed efficiently."

To the extent that political party labels and preferences reflect theoretical understanding of how society works and how to address its problems, the nonpartisan approach further exacerbates the work in the
political laboratory. Strictly speaking, garbage is garbage. But whether
garbage should be dumped efficiently or recycled and whether or not
there ought to be subcontracting of garbage collection to the private
sector—especially when such privatization will substantially reduce the
wages of garbage workers—constitute difficult policy choices that are
not at all obvious. Cities with partisan elections and elected officials
with political frameworks reflecting different political understandings
of the impact of public policies likely respond to the issue of garbage
collection differently than officials in cities without partisan political
orientations. In the latter case, officials enter the laboratory with fewer
analytical tools at their disposal.

POLICIES TO ADDRESS THE PROBLEM OF HOMELESSNESS

The problems faced by local officials in making public policy are well
illustrated by the issue of homelessness and the way in which it is
addressed in city hall. Approaches to the problem of homelessness reflect well the difficulties and frustrations experienced by those who
make policy decisions for their communities. Examining how policies
are formulated to address successfully the issue of homelessness and its

effects on a community shows the consequences of dealing with societal problems under conditions of a lack of control, limited understanding, and difficulties involved with working within the information gap. This area of policy making also exemplifies the difficulties faced by elected officials when empathy, trust, and understanding are in decline in the political system.

The Nature of the Problem

The war against homelessness is now nearly two decades old. As the social safety net decreased in the 1980s and as wages began to decline, the problem of homelessness skyrocketed to the top of the public policy agenda in most urban areas. This problem, like most others, had no single, simple cause and no single, simple solution. Further adding to the difficulty of creating public policies to deal with homelessness was an initially negative, simple, and rigid perception on the part of most citizens about who the homeless were and why they were on the street. The homeless population turned out to be far more diverse than most people's perception of the homeless.

There has always been a homeless problem in the modern American city: Many people without the means to find low-cost dwellings ended up on the streets or in single-room-occupancy (SRO) hotels. As long as SROs were available, this housing option reduced the problem of shelter faced by many people. However, as SROs disappeared, usually due to revitalization efforts in the downtowns of urban areas, large numbers of homeless people were now confronted with life on the street. While data are sketchy, information from the city of Chicago is quite revealing about what was happening in large cities: In 1955, of the people found who were in dire need of shelter, 86 percent lived in SROs. Thirty years later, 12 percent lived in SROs. Between 1955 and 1985, the SRO rooms available in Chicago had declined by 95 percent.[29]

The problem of finding housing for the poor was greatly compounded by policies and actions at all levels of government, which when combined led to a dramatic decline in low-income housing stock from the 1970s through the 1980s. According to some estimates, 2.5 million low-income housing units disappeared after 1980, and by the end of that decade, nearly twice as many low-income families were looking for housing as there were available units. Part of the problem centered on the increased inflationary costs of housing. In the thirteen-year period ending in 1983, rents increased by about 190 percent around the nation, while the income of tenants increased by less than 100 percent, with the result that the costs of housing were taking a larger chunk out of the family budget.[30] Meanwhile, the federal government's response to these needs was minimal at best. The Department of Housing and Urban Development's low-income housing starts declined from about 183,000 units at the start of the 1980s to fewer than 30,000 in 1985.

The decline of single-room-occupancy hotels, the decline in low-income housing stock, and the spiraling costs of rental housing tell only a part of the homelessness story. There were many other factors at work that led to massive increases in the number of homeless on the streets of America, since even by rigorous and conservative counts the problem of homelessness increased fourfold through the 1980s.

A major reason, albeit not the only one, for the increased numbers of homeless on the streets of America's cities was the result of changing economic circumstances that wreaked havoc with the lives of those who lived at the lower end of the economy. Many of the homeless found themselves on the streets as a result of changes in their personal finances—the loss of a job, the disappearance of a second earner in the family, or other personal catastrophes with economic consequences. In the four-year span between 1979 and 1983, the unemployment rate in the United States jumped from 5.8 percent to 9.6 percent. In the longer term, between 1969 and 1989, the numbers of married working-age men without paid work during the calendar year doubled in size and grew by nearly as much for men who were unmarried (and who therefore lacked another source of income). Likewise, single mothers with children and personal incomes below $2,500 had increased by 14 percent in the ten years between 1979 and 1989. In one extensive study of the homeless, over half found themselves on the streets as a result of economic dislocations occurring during the late 1970s through the mid-1980s.[31]

Many of the homeless found themselves without shelter for reasons other than economics. Some were on the street as a result of decisions made by the courts and state legislatures to defund and restructure state mental health hospitals. As many as one-third of the homeless—at least those who had been examined by clinicians—had been diagnosed as having severe mental disorders, and perhaps as many as one-quarter of all homeless would have been in mental institutions had such facilities not been restructured by the legal system.

Some of the homeless ended up on the street as a result of being drug and alcohol abusers. Perhaps as many as one-third of the homeless fit this category if the studies in New York City and other major metropolitan areas can be generalized to other cities.

Other problems related to homelessness are more difficult to address with a clear statistical base. Some of the homeless were Vietnam War veterans no longer able to cope with their personal life circumstances. Some, particularly women with children, were fleeing horrendous family circumstances involving forms of intrafamily violence and often were hiding from homeless men.

Finally, some homeless chose not to work or not to have a "typical" lifestyle. As with other subgroups, it is extremely difficult to gauge the numbers in this category of homeless. One study of Austin's homeless population estimated this subgroup's size as less than 7 percent of the homeless.[32]

Unfortunately, the last group was the easiest to find: relatively young, strong, wearing backpacks and looking menacing. This image on television quickly formed a large part of the homeless stereotype in the minds of the viewing public. When coupled with another group of "drunken," unshaved men sleeping on grates or begging for cash, the two groups of homeless were seen by the public as dangerous and menacing, a problem to be disposed of by municipal government. The victims of domestic violence, entire families sleeping in abandoned cars, and the men and women caught in the Catch-22 of not being able to hold a job because they had nowhere to sleep and to stay clean were seldom seen.

The circumstances leading to the increasing numbers of homeless on the streets of America were quite diverse. Local policy makers were forced to confront four broad types of problems in their communities related to the issue of homelessness. First, activist groups—sometimes including the increasingly politicized homeless—and sympathetic citizens pressured government to provide assistance to the homeless population. Irrespective of the pressure imposed on them by these groups, many policy makers also felt the need to respond to the short-term emergency needs of shelter and housing and to search for long-term solutions to the problem. Many elected officials and citizens see their city as a unique place where people are afforded real opportunities for a good life. People living in public under the most wretched of circumstances (on park benches, on iron grates, in cardboard boxes) challenge the basic perceptions held by citizens about the value of their own community.

A second problem erupted from a different segment of the community: As the issue of homelessness became more visible, municipal officials were confronted with growing demands by citizens and businesses to "eliminate" the perceived threat of homeless people loitering, invading neighborhoods and shopping areas, and threatening adults and children alike. Some businesses felt that customers were deterred by aggressive panhandling and that their businesses suffered financially from the "menacing" environment created by unhealthy-looking stragglers around their establishments. Neighborhood organizations spoke in fear for their children and their property. Local news shows highlighted assaults and robberies involving "transients."

The third problem had its roots in both the nature of the issue and the fiscal context in which municipal officials were operating. Ultimately, homelessness could not be effectively addressed without some combination of short-term emergency assistance and long-term solutions, which, when combined, would impose formidable costs on local governments. Yet any large-scale program, coming at a time of increased burdens (as the federal government was devolving its responsibilities to the local level), was bound to meet substantial opposition from other groups in the community, especially from those who were negatively impacted by growing fiscal problems and who came to feel that scarce resources should not be spent on "transients."

The word *transient* alludes to a fourth problem: How do you tackle a national issue at the municipal level? Many citizens argued that while the community had a responsibility for dealing with its own, policy makers had no right to create programs for "transients" who had come to their city seeking assistance and had further magnified the problem. Thus the extent to which the homeless were local in origin became an issue of considerable controversy in many cities. Due to this problem, any action taken by government would have to face the hurdle of overcoming potential public wrath and loss of support for public policies if it started to look as though the city was becoming more attractive for transients. Policy makers had to devise solutions that would effectively address the problem without impacting negatively on other vital experiments in the political laboratory, and in a manner that would not be attractive to homeless elsewhere.

What to Do?

What do you do when social service agencies demand help for the homeless, neighborhood associations want the transients out of their neighborhoods, businesspeople want loitering to stop, parents fear for the safety of their children, and churches demand help for those down on their luck? And what do you do when you know that thousands of other problems compete for the city's scarce resources, but you also know that a city cannot survive when it is cruel and spiteful to those who need help the most?

You look for answers. But what dimension of the problem to tackle? Here are some options for policy makers:

- Focus solely on the "transient/loitering" problem. Traditionally, this is a police response. City government can pass aggressive anti-panhandling and anti-loitering ordinances, and force the police department to enforce them. The fiscal costs are minimal; all that is needed is to redeploy police officers across the city. The nonfiscal cost of this action, however, is far from negligible. Most police forces are spread rather thin. In our city, we are roughly 150 officers below what is needed for decent responses to emergencies. Such redeployment will impact negatively on responses to burglaries, robberies, and traffic emergencies. Furthermore, the police are extremely unhappy about "transient assignments," and police morale will diminish. Clearly, this strategy will please some neighborhoods and businesses in the short run (the homeless will shift into other neighborhoods and business districts), but there is little hope here for a long-term solution.
- Pursue "exit" strategies. These strategies are designed to get homeless people out of the community. Separate from their ethical implications, these strategies are typically unsuccessful. They specify virtually no services for the homeless (including emergency feeding and housing services), aggressive police response, and moderate funding to pay for bus tickets out of town. In the long run, cities will be tempted to retaliate by sending their homeless to the cities from which other homeless have been driven.
- Engage in "minimalist strategies." These strategies are designed to provide minimum humanitarian assistance to the homeless, at the

least possible cost. Emergency food services are provided for those in desperate need of food, and short-term emergency housing is provided for those in need of shelter. These programs are not inexpensive. Emergency food and housing programs can run annually in the millions of dollars for a medium-sized city and much more for a large city. But there are other costs as well: Typically cities are short on housing programs for poor families, and funding for homeless programs competes with programs to house the poor. Also, both the food and shelter programs need to be located where they are accessible to the homeless. This means that large numbers of the homeless will congregate in the downtown area (that's where most of the bus service is available), impacting heavily on local businesses and surrounding neighborhoods.

One variant of this strategy is to "disperse" emergency services by providing food and housing programs across various sites around the community. This way the impact on one area is minimized but the costs of dispersing the services skyrocket, and now numerous neighborhoods and hundreds of businesses are complaining.

- In contrast to the above choices, the city can always pursue a "comprehensive strategy." This one makes the most sense, and typically it is the hardest one to apply. It forces policy makers to address the diverse nature of the homeless population. To have a comprehensive strategy requires the following:

1. Emergency food and housing facilities for those on the edge of survival.
2. Counseling programs for those who are willing to make a commitment to be mainstreamed back into society.
3. Detox and treatment programs for those with alcohol and drug addictions.
4. Mental health programs for those with illnesses.
5. Employment skills training programs for those with inadequate skills to apply for jobs.
6. Temporary housing for those who secure jobs.

The comprehensive strategy clearly requires a commitment on the part of the homeless to be mainstreamed. For those who choose not to do so, there is a separate door leading to emergency shelter and food but to no other services, coupled to stricter panhandling and loitering ordinances.

This strategy is by far the most expensive one. It will probably work, all other things being equal, but it requires a comprehensive approach and a thoroughness of commitments that will tax the resources of any city. The emergency part of the project is expensive enough. Once other aspects kick in, they test greatly the human resources capabilities of government.

It is not likely that a city will be able to pursue a comprehensive strategy of dealing with homelessness. Currently, there are insufficient funds in most cities to provide drug and alcohol rehabilitation counseling for permanent residents—how would we find the resources for the homeless people in our midst? Job training funds have been devastated by the federal government, and local jurisdictions have had a limited amount of additional tax dollars to invest in job training. How can a city now pit its own poor against the homeless for these limited opportunities? In my city, there is a waiting list of 2,500 families for low-income housing, and these families have been waiting for such housing for over two years. We have 2,500 families on our waiting list because we cut off the list after the first 2,500 applications, and we have little idea of how many more are waiting in the wings. Our housing department has estimated that as many as 25 percent of our families live in substandard housing. Do we shove them aside to provide transitional housing for the homeless people we are trying to mainstream?

Finally, where are the jobs? In my city, the jobs that are available and that pay wages sufficient to get out of poverty either require a college education (or more) or are already taken. One-third of our citizens already work full-time and survive with low-wage jobs only because their spouses work full-time as well. Many of the homeless have no spouses. If they take these jobs, they will remain poor and won't be able to secure housing, find adequate means of transportation, or buy the clothes necessary to keep their jobs.

Even if sufficient resources were available to tackle the problem, the city is nevertheless confronted with the usual problems of making policy. First, there is a great information gap on the issue. Even as fundamental a question as "How many homeless people are there in our city?" often cannot be answered. The homeless are not easily counted. A census can be taken in shelters and food centers, but these counts identify only part of the homeless population, and distort the picture. Homeless families seldom come to shelters. Battered women stay away from places frequented by homeless men. Homeless people who are addicts or who have mental illnesses may not find the shelters. Some who are neither can't get there due to transportation problems. No wonder, then, that in our city, estimates of the homeless ranged from 800 to 3,000 people on any given day. People who wanted the homeless out of the community would underestimate their numbers; often social service agencies, in desperate need of resources, would overestimate the numbers. Furthermore, there was no way to determine how much the ranks of the homeless would grow over the years.

It is no less difficult to uncover what worked and what didn't work elsewhere. Some cities bought "transients" one-way bus tickets, but such actions didn't seem to thin the ranks of the homeless in their communities. Other cities withheld assistance to the homeless, hoping that the word would go out that they were unfriendly to "transients," but there didn't seem to be much evidence that their strategies succeeded in deterring the homeless from migrating there. Still other cities used a warehousing strategy, providing a centralized emergency food and shelter facility for a limited number of days. This answer didn't seem to have an impact on the problem, either. Many cities talked about a comprehensive strategy, but few, if any, had the resources to implement it, and we know too little about the relative success of this type of approach. In short, while the problem of homelessness exists in virtually every city in America, there is no systematic way in which to learn what worked and what didn't.

The cities lacked as well a comprehensive understanding of the problem. While the experts could tell us about the various causes of homelessness, there was no clear explanatory framework with which to guide policy makers in finding an answer. Instead, simplistic theories proliferated. One was the theory of "self-destruction." According to this idea, people were homeless because they were lazy and all they needed to do was to get a job to rid themselves of their homelessness. A second was the "no-fault" theory, as in "It's not my fault that they are homeless, and I shouldn't have to take the risk of them ruining my business [or neighborhood or kid's school]." A third theory was one of "denial." This one held that homelessness was a national problem (all too true), required a national solution (true as well), and could be ignored without guilt as long as local officials lobbied Congress and the White House about the problem. Unfortunately, the problem wouldn't go away. There was even a theory of "callousness." This one argued that the lack of resolution to the homeless problem was due to the lack of caring by policy makers. Those who held to this belief felt that public officials showed their lack of caring through their willingness to spend funds on economic development, roads, the arts, and police, but not on relieving the plight of the homeless.

What would a comprehensive understanding for this problem look like? It would develop a good explanation of the multicausal nature of homelessness and then not only develop multiple strategies to address those causes but also find financial and social mechanisms for their implementation. Equally important, such a theory would address how the remaining functions for governing a city would continue to work while resources were reprioritized and/or newly generated for this problem.

Of course, there is no such pattern of comprehensive understanding anywhere in our cities. There might be, if all the collective experiences with homelessness across the urban landscape would be systematically studied and could be understood and then translated into the individual contexts of each urban area. There is no mechanism to make that happen, and no city could undertake the task for itself. Instead, each city strikes out on its own, learning a little from others and experimenting with policy options in more of a vacuum than is advisable.

Our city first took the hard road of ignoring the problem. That obviously failed as neighborhoods, fearful parents, and businesses came to feel that they were being inundated by homeless people. Then we shifted to the twin strategies of providing emergency assistance and pressuring the federal government to do something about the problem of homelessness. The federal government was sympathetic but largely uninterested. The food and emergency shelter programs were overwhelmed by the number of homeless coming off the streets. We seemed to be churning our wheels while pressure continued to mount from affected social service agencies, businesses, and neighborhoods to "do something."

Finally, we embarked on a "comprehensive strategy": It meant working in partnership with nonprofit organizations, churches, other governments, and the public. Emergency assistance facilities were continued but were dispersed to minimize the effects on any single neighborhood or business area. Now, though, the emphasis was placed on mainstreaming the homeless. Additional funding was secured for counseling services, including detox and rehabilitation programs for drug and alcohol addiction. Resources were redeployed for job training and apprenticeship programs for those who could work. Good samaritans in the community raised money privately to help us. A media "blitz" was created to inform the public of the community effort at mainstreaming. Church leaders spoke out in churches and synagogues about our collective public responsibilities. We were successful in generating a number of federal and private grants.

What type of feedback did the elected officials receive for their efforts? Throughout the entire process, the flow of feedback stayed relatively the same. Neighborhoods that were less stressed now that services were more dispersed nevertheless continued to demand the end of homeless services near them. Businesses continued to cry out against panhandlers and "transients" around their establishments. Social service agencies politely thanked the city council for the additional support but insisted that it wasn't enough, and perhaps there wasn't enough caring about the problem. Churches fought with one another and with government about how much they should help. The homeless were encouraged by their advocates to form a union; they did, and would come and demand more assistance from the city council. It became increasingly difficult to determine whether the enormous efforts undertaken by the city's government benefited anyone.

How successful was the city? Many people were helped. The homeless were fed, and during cold nights shelter was available to all. Many were "mainstreamed" into real jobs. Some kicked booze and drugs, and others left town. Yet after ten years of constant attention to the problem, there is a collective sense of failure. There are perhaps twice as many homeless in the city today as there were ten years ago. The number of homeless people at food facilities is larger than ever before. The shelters are full. The ranks of homeless on street corners, begging for money, seem to overwhelm the city and its residents. If you walked into our community for the first time, you would wonder if anyone has ever done anything about this problem. A little while ago, the city made a national advocacy group's "top ten list" of cruel and uncaring cities for passing an anti-panhandling ordinance.

What went wrong? Part of the answer lies in the problem of lack of control. Most decisions about social policies make assumptions about "all things being equal"; unfortunately, all things are not equal. Although the comprehensive strategy was the best one available, it could not control for continuing changes in the national economy. As our city was fighting the homelessness problem, economic changes involving downsizing, part-time employment, and reduced real wages only served to create more homeless, and the ranks of homeless grew at a faster pace than ever. Nor could the city control decisions made at the national political level, decisions that would create more homelessness. For example, reducing (and in some cases eliminating) the federal social safety net led to many more homeless, including homeless women with children. The greater numbers were bound to overwhelm our modest efforts.

And our efforts were modest. As important as this issue is, it is not the only problem being addressed by policy makers. Only modest resources were reprioritized and spent on the issue. This was a conscious choice for elected officials. They could have spent tens of millions more on the homeless solution but only at the cost of reducing virtually all other important services being provided to the community. Once officials chose to limit the scope of their actions, the solution was doomed at the outset, if success is defined by whether the problem has disappeared.

After a decade of hard work, many millions of dollars of investment, and great conflicts between major segments of the community over how to handle the problem of homelessness, the city has come full circle. For every homeless person who has made it out into the world of work and housing, many more have taken his or her place. Neigbhorhoods still fear for the safety of their children, and many businesspeople decry more than ever the panhandling in front of their establishments. In the great crucible of public policy experimentation, this one has failed at the local level.

Yet there should be a footnote to the failure. The governing body of the city failed but not because it lacked compassion, or caring, or dedication to the problem. It worked on the problem as hard as it could, committed all the resources it felt were available, and tried hard to become innovative and productive. It did most, if not all, of the things we want our public officials to do. Unfortunately, it battled with weapons that were too small against forces that were too large. It never received credit for trying to do the best under arduous circumstances. Only those who worked closely with the council on the problem learned to appreciate the caring and hard work that went into the effort. The rest of the community resigned itself to failure in policy, and came to think less of its government.

8

The Media and City Hall

Fact: In 1998, meeting in Las Vegas, the National Association of Broadcasters inducted Rush Limbaugh into its Hall of Fame.

Democracy makes strong demands on the political system. It requires public officials to be transparent and relatively effective. It requires policy outcomes to generally reflect demands from citizens. It requires bureaucrats to enforce laws both effectively and impartially. Democracy makes demands as well on two other groups: the media and citizens. Citizens must judge the results of the experiments by forming impressions of what is going on in the laboratory of politics and, in response to those impressions, voicing their judgments at the time of elections. Those judgments are critically dependent on the willingness of voters to carefully scrutinize what officials are and are not doing in the political laboratory.

Of course, voters do not have the time or the energy (and probably not the interest) to scrutinize directly the actions of their representatives. Their judgments are made in other ways. Sometimes judgments result from a limited type of direct contact with government: a letter sent to an elected official that is not answered, a rude official in city hall who is dismissive of a phone call, a police officer who responds with courtesy (or lack of it) during a traffic stop. Sometimes the judgments are made through indirect contact: friends, relatives, and colleagues who talk about their direct experiences with government. Most likely, however, judgments about politics and government are made using a combination of both forms of contact plus the impressions citizens gain from news coverage of the political process. Since both direct and indirect contacts with politics are relatively rare for most voters, the media become a critical source of impressions for citizens about the effectiveness of public policies and about the performance of their officials (or lack thereof).

The news media generally have three types of effects on their viewers: agenda setting, cue giving, and issue framing. With respect to agenda setting and cue giving (by highlighting certain issues at the expense of others), the media provide some sense of which issues are important and which are unimportant, and what officials are or are not doing in the political laboratory. For example, a steady diet of drive-by shootings, burglaries, and car-jackings on the local news programs highlights the importance of crime on the public agenda. Likewise, such stories—when unaccompanied by what law enforcement and elected officials are doing about the problem—may provide cues for citizens about the ineffectiveness of government in dealing with communitywide problems.

Issue framing can occur as well. Take as an illustration the problem of low-paying jobs. A series of stories focusing on this problem may highlight it to the viewing public, and the public may place the problem high on its agenda of issues facing the community. Yet the issue may carry little political relevance to viewers unless it is framed in a particular context. Suppose that the story is "framed" in the context of economic development strategies pursued by city officials and the extent to which they spend money attracting the type of industry that has a minimal impact on low wages. In this way, the issue is framed to make it politically relevant and to create a greater possibility that viewers will begin to hold officials responsible for the nature of their local economy.

Citizens, in turn, have potential access to a bewildering array of sources should they wish to survey their political environment. At all levels of government, voters can tune in live and avoid any "translation" by the media. Most city council chambers are now "wired," providing not only gavel-to-gavel coverage of all council meetings on cable television but also "replays" on subsequent nights. The audience for such programming is extremely small and virtually undetectable by ratings agencies.

Most citizens receive their news as translated for them by radio, television and newsprint sources, and it is television news that functions as the most used source for information about politics and public policy.

Through the advent of cable channels, television offers a vast range of news programs at the national level. Complementing the cacophony of both hard news and softer news "programs," the Internet provides further news and commentary on myriad Web pages that reflect newspapers, wire services, newsmagazines, and television programs.

Finally, there is still the "old-fashioned" newspaper. Although most cities have lost the competitive environment of morning and evening local newspapers, at least one solid newspaper exists in most major cities. It is typically complemented by national newspapers—ranging from the *Wall Street Journal* and the *New York Times* to *USA Today*—that are available locally via same-day delivery or the Internet.

Clearly, there is no paucity of either national or local news sources available to interested citizens. The larger question, however, is whether there is news that is actually useful to citizens in making judgments about what elected officials are doing inside the political laboratory. While there is greater competition than ever before between and within news media, such competition does not automatically create quality news products. In fact, it may create the opposite. In an increasingly competitive market, pressures to succeed financially may alter the news product dramatically. Getting to be first in audience ratings on television likely requires a visually exciting—or truly sensational—product regardless of its actual news value. Newspapers, in competition with other newsprint, television, and the Internet, are under financial pressure to reduce the number of column inches devoted to news in favor of advertising. Worse yet, to compete with television, they have to provide a visually attractive package, one shorter on news and longer on color and pictures (a product pioneered by *USA Today*).

So television has come to dominate the news media, and its format has forever restructured the way we get our news. Yet television is also in a process of major change. Technology—in the form of both cable and Internet services—is changing television viewing habits, with the practical outcome that the traditional broadcasters are losing their audiences as those audiences disperse across a nearly infinite visual spectrum. While television news through the major networks and their affiliates still remains the primary source of information for most citizens, the network audience is shrinking dramatically. When the president of the United States holds a televised news conference, it is probably seen by 60 percent fewer American viewers than it would have been the case twenty-five years ago. This is how much the captive audience of network television has shrunk in the last quarter century. Likewise, when a local station covers the news about the city council, its audience is dramatically smaller than it has been in recent times.

This change has made the lives of public officials more difficult. To do their jobs well—which includes communicating with the public about what they are doing and why—now requires unusual efforts to get on television to make their views heard. Equally important, less access to the public means that citizens themselves are less likely to see and understand what their officials do, and they have fewer cues about judging their representatives.

This assumes, that is, that all else is equal: that the media are endeavoring to report what is actually happening in the political laboratory. That, unfortunately, is not the case. In fact, the responsible citizen watching the news may find it very difficult to ascertain what her representatives are doing. Failing to report, or reporting without context, may do significant damage to the political process. Here is one illustration: Recently, both the president and the majority in Congress released their budget recommendations. PBS set aside fifteen minutes—an eternity on television—for the subject on its nightly newscast. A very short report was followed by a long analysis. The analysis consisted of a moderator and two partisans representing their respective political parties. The viewing public was then treated to charges and countercharges between partisans about the inaccuracies of the "other side's" description of the alternatives. Understanding the actual differences between the two proposals would have required the audience to read the five budget books that were the subject of debate. Clearly unavailable during the broadcast was a third-party analysis of the competing options. Others things were available, though: rancor, anger, and charges and countercharges of mismanagement and deception. Rather than learning anything about budget alternatives or how each group wanted to prioritize America's problems, it would have taken the most generous citizen to conclude anything other than that mean little children were at play in a sandbox.

Of course, this image didn't occur by accident; it was designed. The segment was "framed" by the news producer, who had a variety of choices in presenting the story but chose to do it in a "conflicts caused by partisan wrangling" context. And true to the theme, the moderator—turning from one advocate to the other—would egg on the contestants with taunts of "Is that correct?" or "How do you feel about that?" All in all, it was fair drama, but it in no way resembled hard news, and it created the wrong impression of what was actually going on in the political laboratory: conflicts of values over policy priorities. This coverage represented the in-depth version of the news about the budget. The main networks simply relied on party and White House spokespeople for quick, positive comments about their versions of the budget. The networks' stories on this topic lasted less than two minutes, and virtually nothing was discussed about alternative budgetary priorities.

Things are not all that different at the local level except that the coverage of the political laboratory is even more spotty than at the national level. Local news, unlike its national counterpart, is longer (often one and a half hours in the evening) but is filled with items other than local news: national and international news "time bites" and "teasers" from the networks, weather, and sports along with a daily diet of feature stories of "local interest." Often in an hour and a half of local news there is less local news than there is national and international news in a half hour of a network's national news program.

Consequently, local officials must worry about a number of problems in trying to communicate with their constituents. First, knowing that television is the primary news source, they must somehow be able to communicate through a visual medium. Television has little tolerance for "talking heads." Simply talking at the camera creates little excitement and drama and is visually uninteresting. While the news broadcast will run a panoramic view of the city council chambers, seldom will the camera pause long enough to pick up a major statement of policy by a council member or mayor unless it is very dramatic (outrageous?) or is accompanied by some animated gestures. Even under such circumstances, it is relatively rare for television news to cover city council events. Meetings are long and agendas are complex. No television crew will sit for hours to get thirty seconds or a minute of interesting footage. Complicating this problem is another: Unlike newspaper reporters, most television reporters do not have a "beat" or an area of specialization. They are generalists by training and have a difficult time ascertaining which parts of the council meeting are likely to be exciting, dramatic, or highly salient for the public. Given these limitations of television, officials must engage in "affirmative action" if they wish to communicate with voters through television news. Affirmative action can take many forms, but all involve trying to convince television reporters about the importance of their actions and at a specific time during the meeting. Such affirmative action borders on media manipulation and is likely to be resented by television news producers. In turn, resentful news producers don't cover the object of their resentment. No wonder, then, that officials engaging in "affirmative action" don't get on television news very often.

Newspapers pose a different problem for officials. Newspaper reporters do specialize; an unfortunate reporter may have city hall as her "beat" for years. They also prepare for council meetings, read agenda materials, and are forced to sit through hours of meetings every week. Their responsibility, however, is not only to cover the news but also to stay within the confines of what their city editors believe people will be interested in reading. One veteran—and highly successful—reporter told me his formula: "Taxes and sex. If I can get both in the story, people will read it and it will be front page. Sex alone may make front page; a story on taxes going up will have some good chance. If both are out, it isn't going to be read and will barely survive getting in the paper." Regardless of whether such "rules" of coverage accurately reflect reader interest—and I suspect they do not—as long as editors and reporters conform to them, they will drive the content of coverage.

What will also drive the content of newspaper coverage is brevity: There just isn't all that much space available for news stories in local newspapers. They are increasingly preempted by visuals (color pictures and graphs to compete with television) and huge amounts of advertising. The space issue means that even if a reporter wants to cover matters other than tax and sex stories, there will be very little space to go into coverage that is in-depth and reflective of what most officials are doing around the council table.

What does all this mean to the elected official? She has two basic strategies: One is to let the story come to her—that is, to assume that the issue she wants to talk about is going to be of such great import that the reporter will be forced to cover both it and her activities. But she runs a great risk in pursuing this strategy, because if it fails to work, she will get little coverage, leading to an inability to communicate with the public, and worse—with no coverage, citizens will come to believe that she is either ineffective or doing nothing.

The other strategy is a limited form of "affirmative action": You bide your time and don't speak very often, but when you do speak you engage in drama of the type sought by the reporter ("This action will raise taxes for our people," or "Your bill will force seniors out of their homes by raising taxes"). This type of drama often leads to strong negative responses by colleagues around the table, escalating conflicts between policy makers and reducing the ability to get much done in the political laboratory. There is another cost to engaging in this strategy: You will quickly get the label of "grandstander" and may pay the price of being shut out of the decision-making process altogether by other council members.

Both strategies are fraught with great risks, so local officials most often settle for trying to cultivate a good relationship with the beat reporter in hopes of "getting a break" while continuing to go about the task of formulating public policy around the council table. In doing so, they recognize that their actions will not be well covered and the public will seldom know what they have done in a given day, how much they have worked to get there, or the context in which they have made decisions. Nor can they do what politicians do at the national level, because they lack the resources available to their national counterparts. Members of Congress have extensive franking privileges, allowing them to send out letters to their constituents, and even "newsletters" to all voters in the district, on a regular basis. In addition, they employ people full-time whose job is to work the media to get their bosses on the air and in the newspapers. Local officials, more than any other political group, are dependent on the vagaries of the media to communicate with the public about their positions and the issues facing their communities.

How successful are they? This is an extremely difficult question to answer as success depends in part on a range of idiosyncratic considerations. How smart is the official in understanding the dynamics of news coverage? How honest and open is he in dealing with news gatherers? How flexible is he in adapting to the varied needs of both television and newspaper reporters? How hard is he willing to work to communicate through the media? How much is he willing to reprioritize limited time for these efforts?

There are, however, some noticeable patterns to news coverage at the local level that transcend the idiosyncracies of the newsmakers. These patterns can be uncovered through a careful scrutiny of media coverage (called content analysis) and a comparison of the coverage with the actual raw events being covered. I've done so on several occasions, over time and across local jurisdictions, and I find the patterns to be fairly consistent across the cities of our nation.

WHAT'S GOING ON AT CITY HALL?

The description that follows is fairly typical of the type of news coverage experienced by local officials who work in the political laboratory. Let's set the scene first. It is a Monday in the spring toward the end of the 1990s in a city of about 750,000 citizens. As in most cities, the council's day will consist of a "study session," an "executive session," and a "regular meeting." The meetings start around noon, will break from 5:00 to 7:00 P.M., and then resume until 10:30 P.M. or later. The regular meeting is for formal public hearings and for official voting on laws and ordinances, most of which were massaged and discussed extensively in previous weeks' study sessions. This part of the meeting is typically held in the evening to allow citizens to attend after work. Even when there are formal public hearings, they seldom result in the enactment of laws. The feedback from them is discussed in future study sessions, leading to modifications of the original ordinance.

The study session is where the political laboratory is at its most interesting: This is where the mayor and council members roll up their sleeves, confront each other's policy views, and try to hammer out directions for policies and ordinances that will be enacted in upcoming regular sessions. The executive session is reserved for discussion of ongoing litigation and is conducted behind closed doors, the one piece of the political laboratory sealed from the scrutiny of citizens and media. In fact, in most cities it is illegal (a misdemeanor or a felony) for those attending the executive session to discuss publicly anything about the proceedings.

News, in its strict definition, is meant to be unique, unpredictable, important, and available for relatively accurate[33] coverage (and for television, accessible for visual coverage). Obviously, importance is a perceptual phenomenon, and reporters and editors develop procedures for identifying what is important. Predictability, though, is something that can be identified relatively objectively. If you know that every Monday at noon the mayor will denounce the city council as useless and irresponsible, then the event becomes predictable and is not news. If it fails to happen, then its failure may be unique, unpredictable, and therefore within the context of what is meant by news.

Quite clearly, an executive session should be a prime subject for news. It is typically unique, deals with subjects that are unpredictable (as in, "If we could have predicted this, we wouldn't be getting sued [or wouldn't be suing]"), and is often exciting (involving someone or some group that has made large mistakes, and consequently these mistakes are about to cost taxpayers money). Unfortunately, it is the worst context for news—inaccessible and nonvisual (no cameras allowed, not even talking heads after the session)—and reporters can only guess at what has transpired. Even the occasional public action (involving an ordinance that, for example, frees up money for litigation or a settlement) is so obscure as to make the story virtually incomprehensible.

Thus, executive sessions either are not covered by local news sources or are covered on a very limited basis and often inaccurately (with the reporter guessing about the outcome of the closed session). When the coverage is inaccurate, local officials must suffer the slings and arrows of a public unhappy with their "decisions" without clarification or response since they are not allowed to reveal the contents of these discussions.

These are not problems faced in covering study or regular sessions. But in those sessions, a whole host of other problems arise, ranging from too much activity to too little specialization on the part of those covering the events. We should expect, then, that the coverage—even when well-meant and done by competent professionals—will greatly distort the public's view of what is going on in the political laboratory, diminish the ability of citizens to make competent judgments about their elected officials, and make it extremely difficult for local politicians to communicate meaningfully with citizens about what they do and why they do it.

The particular city we are discussing here is typical in terms of media outlets. It has four television stations with daily local news programs. In addition, there are two daily newspapers covering events of local importance. On this particular day, the city council will have a full, albeit not overwhelming, agenda on its hands. Two issues will be discussed in executive session; the study session has eleven items; and the regular session has only sixteen items on the calendar. All items have been publicly advertised, and well in advance of the meeting. The agendas have been posted in hard copy and electronically on the city's Web page. Reporters and interested citizens had access to accompanying agenda materials (except for the executive session) days in advance of the meeting. Reporters have no surprises in store for them and could have prepared in advance to cover what they deemed to be "newsworthy" events.

What happened, then, on this particular Monday in the political laboratory, and what was covered? While meeting in executive session, the governing body addressed its two issues. One was a minor lawsuit, resulting in a $30,000 settlement. The city attorney argued that, although the city was not liable, a sympathetic jury for the plaintiff could bring in a judgment five times the size of the proposed settlement, and it was in the interest of the city to accept the offer. A short discussion resulted in unanimous agreement with the city attorney.

The second issue was legal in nature as well but resulted in more explosive debate. This one centered on a contract that was to expire between the city and one of its professional sports teams using city facilities. The team was not producing revenue, and the owners wanted the city government to increase the subsidy for the activity, or they threatened to take the team to another community. After considerable discussion—which included accusations directed at the owners, at one another, and at the city's bureaucracy—the council decided to authorize the city manager to continue to negotiate with the owners in the time still available before the end of the contract.

In study session, the governing body proceeded to other matters. Eleven different matters of varying lengths and salience were discussed. The five most important (at least in terms of issues of high priority and involving substantial fiscal consequences for the community) involved pending federal and state legislation that would negatively impact on the ability of the city to deliver services; the city's approach to the "Y2K" problem; a new strategy for generating health-care benefits for the community's citizens; the role of the city in ensuring an uncontaminated water supply for the region; and a major and controversial rezoning case.

Sixteen items constituted a relatively light agenda for the regular session. These included an advertised public hearing regarding a proposal to increase recreation fees. Some twenty people spoke at the public hearing, and after it closed, the council agreed to study further the information received from citizens before passing any new fees.

In all, the political laboratory was open to the public and the media for eight hours on this given day. Elected officials discussed and cast their preferences on twenty-nine different issues. Before the meeting, these officials spent hundreds of hours in preparation, reading documents and interacting with one another, with their respective staffs, and with city administration. Several consulted with key leaders in the community and talked to numerous citizens who contacted them about various agenda items. Virtually all of them came into these sessions prepared and ready to conduct the experiment. The mayor and a couple of the council members spoke on virtually all of the issues before them. The rest addressed only a few issues, and no one took the lead on more than a couple. Perhaps half the council asserted strongly their policy positions when speaking and engaged in public attempts to influence their colleagues, another quarter spoke only to register the reasons for their positions, and another quarter barely mumbled something when it was their turn to speak. As in all areas of life, considerable diversity was demonstrated across the table. Some worked hard; others less so. Some offered a keen appreciation of problems; others barely understood their own positions. Had the voters been in the laboratory, they would have probably concluded—irrespective of policy agreements with their representatives—that they could take pride in some of their politicians and should be concerned about others.

Of course, very few voters were present in the political laboratory. There were, on this particular day, no more than 80 citizens in attendance at the regular session, and perhaps fewer than 50 at the study session, out of more than 300,000 registered voters. Those who were not there but who would later claim to know what the city council had done came to their beliefs about what went on in the political laboratory through the filtered lenses of television and newspaper coverage.

And what did they learn? On Channel 2, the most-watched television news program in the community, voters saw very little. In ninety minutes of local news (an hour in the early evening and another half hour at the end of prime-time programming), only 14 percent of the stories (three stories in the early evening and three stories later at night) were devoted to the city council. Less than 8 percent of the airtime was spent on what happened at city hall. Even more instructive is the placement of stories. Placement is important: Stories in the first or second segment signify to the viewing public that the story is important. The later segments reflect either triviality or more "features" than hard news. In this community, three of the four local news programs run for a half hour, then break for national news, and then provide another half hour of local news programming. The "hard news" is supposedly contained in the first two segments of the first half. Channel 2 ran thirteen news stories in the first half hour before shifting to weather and sports. There was not a single mention of anything happening in city hall. It was not until the second half-hour segment that mention was made of the political laboratory. The station reported that the council would hold a public hearing that evening on recreation fees (this was not news as much as it was "news that will be happening later"). It reported as well on the rezoning controversy, but since the council did nothing but continue discussion of the issue, the report focused on how angry the two sides were, with each making negative statements about the city council. No council members were interviewed for their response. Finally, a report was given on the unwillingness of the city council to subsidize a request for a celebration downtown.

Video coverage in the interim consisted of a reporter standing in front of city hall, talking about the meeting. This view was interrupted with a brief "sweep" of the study session showing some council members writing, some listening, and one member talking (no audio). None of the three reports differentiated council members from each other; voters couldn't tell if all were in agreement on everything or if different members in the laboratory were taking different approaches to the experiments unfolding.

Channel 2's late-evening coverage was no more enlightening. Sixteen stories were covered, of which three mentioned the city council's activities, but they were the same three that had been covered earlier. The only change was that the advertised public hearing in the earlier program now had turned into a report on the public hearing, with a video clip of two people denouncing the council for proposing a rate increase. The council members were shown listening politely to the citizens' comments.

Channel 4 has the second-most-watched news program in the community. Its coverage was even thinner and less accurate. In its first hour of local news, it had only two stories (15 percent of all news stories) of the council's activities, consuming less than 7 percent of non-commercial time. Unlike the other station, however, it ran both stories in the first segment, indicating that these were important events. The first story was on the executive session, and the reporter—standing in front of city hall—proudly reported the scoop that the council decided behind closed doors that the professional sports team would be kicked out of city facilities. This was followed by citizen interviews both for and against the council's actions. The anchor then also reported that a public hearing was scheduled on fee increases for recreation activities.

It's a good thing that there was no more coverage: The lead story was wrong. The council did not end the contract with the professional team, and unfortunately the station did not retract the story; in fact, quite the opposite—the story played again that evening. It wasn't until two days later that one of the newspapers reported that the contract was still being negotiated by the two sides. This particular news program went on the air with a story it had to guess at, and council members could not respond to the inaccuracies since they could not reveal the content of executive sessions. Consequently, many citizens who liked having the professional team in the city were angered about the public officials' supposed cavalier attitude toward their team and broadly criticized the council for actions they had not undertaken.

Channel 5 spent even less time on the city council than did the other two stations. Its coverage contained the fewest stories on the council (7 percent) and the least airtime (4 percent), reporting only on the conflict over the rezoning case in the study session and about the sports team discussion in the executive session, and repeating the rezoning case issue in its late-night broadcast. At least this station indicated that it did not know what the sports-team decision was or what was specifically discussed.

Channel 8 produces only one-third of the news time of the other channels. It has only a half hour of news in the early evening. On this particular day, it covered eleven stories in depth. Not a single reference was made to the city council. Few watch this station, but no one who did could have discovered by watching it that the council had even met on this day.

What could citizens—whose prime source of news is television—have learned about their representatives and their actions in the political laboratory? Likely the following lessons:

- *Little was being done in the laboratory.* The coverage was minimal and there was little context: None of the reporters gave the background for their stories or the length of time the council spent discussing the items on the agendas.
- *Nothing good comes out of city hall.* Without fail, all the stories were about either inaction on the part of the council (postponing decisions after discussion or public hearing) or proposals for increasing fees or eliminating activities enjoyed by the community.
- *There is little diversity in representation in the laboratory (that is, all politicians are the same).* In actuality, there was considerable disagreement and debate among the members of the council, in both the study session and the regular session. None of it was reported. In fact, none of the votes was reported on television, and only one vote was reported in the morning newspaper. It was impossible for citizens to realize that their own representatives may have behaved differently from the group.

One could plausibly argue that coverage was skimpy and of low priority because other events of great magnitude had crowded out coverage of the political laboratory. This doesn't seem to have been the case. Issues that consumed significantly more airtime and that were given better positioning than the government stories included impending weather changes (during the news, not the weather segment); water conservation and fighting depression; a local baseball player charged with a felony; the release of wolves into the wilderness thousands of miles from the community; the induction of Billy Joel into the Rock and Roll Hall of Fame; and scores of national and international news items (for example, a major car accident in Belgium) that served as teasers for the network's national news program.

Neither is it the case that no major issues of consequence were being addressed by the city council other than those reported. In fact, perhaps the most important issue being discussed was completely ignored. It consisted of a nearly hour-long discussion in the study session of what the city had and had not done about the Y2K problem. The problem itself had been reported—in terms of its national and international scope—for months, both on television and in newsprint. It was clearly an important issue in the minds of editors and news producers, and it was a constant point of concern in citizen forums. Ironically, on the day that the council was handling this issue, two of the four television stations addressed the way the problem was being dealt with in Washington, D.C. (with video from a national feed), and one channel even addressed the problem in the state capital. Both newspapers ran stories (edited versions of wire service stories) about the national approach to the problem. Yet not a mention was made about how the problem was being tackled in the local political laboratory.

Had the local Y2K coverage occurred, citizens could have learned that the city had been addressing the problem for quite some time. It had spent substantial resources on its computers, had commissioned outside consultants to assist it in its work, and had chosen to develop a fool-proof system for confronting the issue. In his final discussion with the council, the consultant identified the activities engaged in by every department dealing with the problem, and the governing body was assured that the city had completely resolved the issue nearly a year before its onset. Citizens could have seen a council that—on this rare occasion—worked smoothly without much conflict, achieved something very important, invested wisely its public resources, and averted a major crisis for the community.

Yet none of those judgments would be forthcoming; there was no coverage. Perhaps there could have been if the members had been smart enough to advertise the issue in very different terms. For example, they could have publicly pressed the idea that their actions had saved millions of tax dollars, or that hundreds—perhaps thousands—of lives were saved by their actions. They didn't. They were too busy doing their jobs and left "issue framing" to the media, and the media chose to ignore the story altogether.

In this community, as in most other cities, television has become the primary source of news for citizens, but it is not the only major source of news. People still read newspapers, and I shouldn't conclude this chapter without mentioning local newsprint coverage of the political laboratory. There indeed was coverage by both newspapers. The morning newspaper on the next day had front-page coverage of the public hearing on the proposed increase in recreation fees, highlighting the anger citizens felt about an increase, providing background on why the fees might be needed, and stating that the council didn't act. The "city" section also carried the story on the continuing discussion of the rezoning case, and underneath it the many hours that the council spent on other issues were awarded single-paragraph "bullets." Out of all the column inches available for news, only 3 percent of news coverage actually focused on the activities of the council, an amount smaller than the airtime afforded by the television stations. The evening paper did worse; it gave only 2.5 percent of its coverage to the activities inside the political laboratory. However, there was plenty of space available in both papers for matters other than news. On average, only 32 percent of each paper was actually used for news; the remainder was primarily for advertising, pictures, editorials, and op-ed pieces. Even some of the news seemed old rather than new: Both newspapers carried wire service stories and feature columns that were reported a day earlier by the *New York Times* and the *Washington Post*.

It is easy to blame the media for such scant and sometimes shoddy coverage of the political laboratory, and perhaps they deserve some of the blame. Unfortunately, news producers and news editors now face forces often beyond their control. Television news at the local level must minimize its costs and maximize its visual value to the audience. The cost problem means not having enough staff to specialize in government issues and not being able to plan sufficiently in advance to create interesting visuals to accompany local government stories. The stations seldom have enough resources to engage in substantial background research, and as a result, they end up guessing about what is happening, what is important, and what consequences come about as a result of public policy decisions. Under strong competitive pressure to reduce costs and to increase ratings, it is easier to minimize stories about the political laboratory and to focus instead on the high "drama" involved with local crimes and accidents. No wonder, then, that many stations invest in helicopters and high technology to "bring you live" a car chase, a flood, or a major accident.

Likewise, newspapers are under immense competitive pressure. They compete today less with each other than with other media, especially television and the Internet. With declining subscriptions, advertising revenue is essential, and advertising crowds out space for news. New technology is used not to bring more accurate news but to generate cleaner, prettier, color pictures and graphics to provide some visual content in the battle with other, largely image-based media. Too often, the least amount of attention and resources is focused on the actual reporters, who are typically substantially underpaid in most cities and who have to fight tooth and nail for sufficient space to report the events in the laboratory.

Politicians are not exactly bystanders in all of this. But they, too, have limited resources, limited time, and sometimes a limited understanding of how the media work. They can influence media coverage and create a stronger spotlight on the laboratory, but only at a substantial cost. To do so, they will alienate some or most of their colleagues, reduce the precious time available to deal with the myriad experiments in the laboratory, and if they hire an expert (that is, a press relations person), they will be accused of wasting precious tax dollars. So, with sporadic attempts to influence the media, they, too, become unwilling participants in a type of coverage that does little to highlight their behavior and the consequences of their actions.

Meanwhile, what is going on in the laboratory is becoming a greater and greater mystery to voters, who must ultimately judge the experimenters' performance. The "learning" that takes place from seeing or reading the news is overwhelmingly negative learning about their government. Virtually no television news program, and only the very rare and compassionate (and virtually nonexistent) newspaper story, ever conveys the hard work, the tough choices, the agony of choosing amongst limited options, or the tremendous worrying about the consequences of policy decisions being played out behind a simple vote on a policy or an ordinance.

No wonder, then, that empathy continues to decline among those who must judge the performance of their officials based on what they view and what they read. Assuming that the forces and dynamics driving both television and newspapers continue in the same direction, there is little hope that the news gatherers will be able to increase empathy in the political culture.

9

Looking for Empathy in American Politics

Where do we go from here? It is clear that without greater empathy on the part of the public toward those who work in the political laboratory, democracy is in trouble. What is there to do? While I hope that this book will increase the dialogue about the problem, I am under no illusion that it can reverse trends that are glacial in strength and direction. We will need many books, many articles, and many discussions before we can change attitudes.

It is also clear that most of the forces that impact on this problem are moving in tandem to continue to reduce rather than increase empathy in American society. Before responding to the question of what new things need to be done, another question should be answered first: Are the trends noted in this book reversible, and if so, how?

It would not be necessary to increase empathy in the American political culture as long as there were other factors operating in the political process that would allow the experimentation in the laboratory to continue in a democratic manner. We know that our form of democracy has survived previously despite low levels of empathy. One possibility is that we can live without more empathy as long as some of the forces that made it possible for the democratic political culture to operate in its absence will return once more to center stage.

One force that in the past mitigated low levels of empathy toward politicians had to do with citizens' strong allegiances to the two political parties. Such allegiances functioned in the past to provide a strong positive attachment to both individual officeholders and the political process irrespective of some significant individual failures (real or perceived) on the part of the politicians in the laboratory. Such strong partisan affiliation has diminished dramatically in recent times.

Can strong partisan allegiance return? I doubt it. On the Republican side, the prospects are grim. The party is strongly divided between its leadership, held captive by its conservative ideological wing, and the rank and file of Republican voters who are much more moderate and pragmatic. As long as the party is trapped between a hard-core ideological group that is unwilling to allow centrists to see themselves as part of the party, it is highly unlikely that the Republican Party will strengthen its identification with a public that is relatively nonideological.

The problems are different on the Democratic side, but the consequences may be the same. The Democrats have lost a large base of support among the public and overwhelmingly from the ranks of those whose participation in politics has shrunk dramatically. These citizens include large numbers of blue-collar workers; low-wage white-collar workers; and minorities. The party offers to many of these citizens a better alternative than the Republicans but not sufficiently so as to reestablish deep loyalties to its increasingly hard to comprehend principles. As the party's conservative wing has pushed it closer to Republican ideas, the intensity of loyalty to the Democratic Party has correspondingly dwindled. Much of this loss of partisan allegiance has been manifested not so much in terms of voting for the other party as in not voting at all or reregistering as an independent.

It seems highly unlikely that the two parties will ever regenerate the types of loyalties they enjoyed even thirty years ago. And the problem is only partly within the politics of each party. The combination of new technologies (for instance, television, the Internet, and new approaches to direct mail campaigns) and new ways of funding campaigns (with campaigns relying overwhelmingly on their own fund-raising capabilities through political action committees) has further atomized both parties, often leaving them at the mercy of their own candidates, who are more interested in winning elections than in rebuilding their respective parties.

It is possible, of course, that party allegiance will reemerge, but it would likely require a wholesale restructuring of political parties. This has happened a number of times in the history of American politics. While third-party movements are almost never successful in the United States, it is plausible that one of the two political parties would collapse and a new party would form to take its place. Certainly the conservative wing of the Republican Party has made noises in this direction. Still, such change is not likely in the near future.

One other change could strengthen political parties: fundamental campaign finance reform. Such change could have two effects. First, it would free both political parties (and their candidates) from the enormous power of very wealthy special-interest groups that now fund so much of national politics. Such freedom could allow both parties to argue much more strongly for public policies needed by many Americans and in so doing reestablish loyalties to the parties. At the grassroots level, the common complaint is that neither the party nor its many candidates truly care about most problems facing citizens, and thus they become indistinguishable from each other.

The second effect would be that fundamental campaign finance reform, by limiting spending and the role of special interests, could once more make the parties important in the eyes of candidates. Candidates who run for election today cultivate their own financial base, and volunteer base as well. As the financial base becomes less important, the power of volunteers once more increases. While candidates can raise a volunteer army over an election cycle, the allegiances they cultivate go not to the party but to the individual candidate. The parties could raise and hold such volunteer cadres on a more permanent basis if they could be freed from the ever-present hunt for more money. The fact that they don't do so now can be attributed to their placing less emphasis on volunteers and more on needed funding. That is not the only reason, though: It is in no small measure due as well to the growing perception that such volunteers are relatively unimportant compared to the power of money. Yet such volunteerism, through the direct involvement of active citizens with political candidates and officials in the trenches, could have a substantial ripple effect in restoring allegiance to the party and could create greater empathy toward those who run and serve. Unfortunately, fundamental campaign finance reform, while a bit more likely to happen than the rejuvenation of the political parties, is still not very likely in the near future.

If the prospect of rejuvenating political parties is not a very good one, then are there other groups who could serve a similar function in creating an alternative to the empathy missing in the political culture? It is possible that we could have something similar to empathy by analogy.

As long as citizens are active in social, cultural, and civic organizations, they may learn to trust one another and to learn about the difficulties of dealing with complex problems (there seems to be some significant relationship between interpersonal trust and political trust, although the two have diverged somewhat in recent times). They may translate such experiences to an understanding of the political arena.

In the past, Americans were known as joiners. They joined civic groups and associations in numbers unheard of in most democratic countries. While there is some disagreement over whether we are participating in fewer and fewer of these types of organizations, the weight of evidence seems to suggest that much of this associational activity is now in decline. This is the reason why so many political scientists worry about the extent to which we have shifted from bowling in leagues to bowling alone. Although actual participation in associations has fallen substantially, more Americans continue to join more associations than citizens in any other country in the world, and this is so across a broad spectrum of groups, including bowling leagues, PTAs, and church groups. Associational involvement, especially involvement that creates the type of impact on the political system I am suggesting here, requires not just joining groups but participating in them. Such participation continues to diminish. Part of the reason is economic—adults are working harder and for more hours to survive even in good economic times, leaving little time for participatory activities outside the home.

Furthermore, participatory activities in the workplace and even in as mundane an activity as shopping are pulling in nonparticipatory directions. Telecommuting, for instance, is on the rise and will substantially increase in American life. Telecommuting will mean fewer face-to-face interactions in the workplace. Likewise, as the Internet increases its scope of services, it will further isolate people from one another as customers will need to make fewer personal, face-to-face contacts with providers of goods and services. It would be wonderful to think that we could restore a world where parents spend more time with other parents at PTA functions and where more people join in evening coffees to talk about newly published novels. These changes, however, are not likely to occur. It is clear that the economy will continue to require both parents to work, leaving much less time and energy for other activities. New technology will only accelerate the trend toward electronic chat rooms and will socialize a new generation of Americans to replacing the living room with the "virtual" room for small-group conversation. It is not likely that Americans will learn to empathize with those working in the political laboratory by seeing the complexities of social problem solving through small groups of social relationships, because they will continue to have fewer such experiences.

Neither can we rely on the media to bring us more empathetic portraits of what goes on inside the political laboratory. With respect to network (and affiliate) television news, the trends point toward continuing desertions by audiences in favor of cable and Internet sources of information. Such trends mean that further cost reductions for news capabilities, coupled with the need for more "creative" and exciting news, will lead to less coverage of the inner workings of the political laboratory. And there is not much hope that cable television will function much better. Although cable carries many more news shows than the networks, most of these are filled with attack journalism: bringing on a representative of a point of view and subjecting this person to attack by journalists. Similar to this format is another: bringing into the studio politicians who occupy extreme positions on a particular issue and encouraging them to go at each other. The growth of these programs seems to suggest that this is the most cost-effective, successful format for cable news programs. Its success may in turn drive the networks to analogous programming (one network—Fox—is already practicing this style of news, and MSNBC and CNN have versions of it on their cable stations). None of these trends augurs well for an empathetic view inside the political laboratory through television, either at the national or the local level.

Some change may be possible at the local level. Citizen activists and concerned citizens can demand more news reporting about their government from local stations. They can demand more in-depth coverage of their local government, and I suspect that at least in medium-size and smaller cities station managers may respond. Station managers in these cities are visible and accessible, and they often engage in civic and charitable activities. Many also believe that they have a responsibility for public service and should be responsive to viewer demands. Such responses will not be forthcoming, however, unless stations hear persistent and strong demands from their audiences. Unfortunately, the

Catch-22 is that such demands are not likely to be heard unless viewers come to understand that what they are seeing is so little of what is actually happening in the political laboratory.

It is much harder to make predictions about the future of newspapers and their coverage of government and politics. It is a persistent bit of good news that journalists still specialize, and many devote themselves to the practice of journalism as a principled career, despite the outrageously low pay. It is true as well that, in addition to expertise, newspapers can add additional space with which to engage in in-depth coverage of the political laboratory. The real question, however, is whether the incentives for this type of coverage—not there now—will emerge in the future. There is certainly significant in-depth coverage today of certain types of issues, but such coverage is driven by guesses at what is exciting and interesting to the reading public, and these guesses usually come down on the side of potential scandal.

The never-ending Monica Lewinsky affair seems to have been unique in scope and consequence but not novel in terms of the media's proclivity for scandal. A prominent journalism professor recently told me that Bob Woodward and Carl Bernstein—the key journalists behind the Watergate story a quarter of a century ago—did more damage to journalism than they helped the cause of justice in America. He argued that their lasting legacy has been a generation of reporters and editors who are "hell bent on exposing more Watergates and their equivalents than is possible to have in our lifetime." "They are trained to report the news and to create a newspaper of record," he said, "but they live to uncover scandal they believe is found in the rooms of political power, and they will search and expose even when there is nothing left to search and expose."

In addition to the Watergate "culture" in journalism today, the difficulties that newspapers face in competing with more visual (television) and interactive (the Internet and "talk radio") media are likely to push them toward essentially mimicking the news seen and heard in the other media. Furthermore, as newspapers continue to be financially challenged, competition among them will diminish even more as morning papers merge with their afternoon brethren. Others will seek to utilize the Internet to fashion interactive relationships with their subscribers and to increase even further their advertising dollars. Even now, many newspapers have entered the Internet game, offering electronic versions of their newspapers, complete with advertisements, chat rooms, and more advertisements. Some even offer e-mail and Web connections for a monthly fee, and through them direct contact to other service providers. In this manner, they compete not only with other newspapers but also with other Internet hosts for advertisements, and they are diversifying rapidly away from the basic business of news gathering.

The eventual integration of newspapers into the Internet will mean that they will be relegated to being just a few of the millions of Web pages available to browsers. Even if we can assume that they will expand their coverage of the political laboratory (after all, there is virtually no space limitation on a newspaper's Internet version), they will never again assume the central place they served in our lives in the twentieth century.

Still, there may be some hope here. The public may have demonstrated a collective revulsion to scandalmongering over the Lewinsky affair, underlined by the fact that with each revelation the president's performance rating in the polls seemed to increase. As the affair receded from the headlines, it was followed by substantial journalistic reexamination of what reporters should pursue. Yet this is but a small ray of hope in a grim set of scenarios about future newspaper coverage of the political laboratory.

If neither party allegiance nor better news coverage is a likely vehicle with which we can increase empathy, then perhaps the politicians working in the laboratory will rechannel some of their energies and behavior to helping to create more empathy for their experiments. After all, they are not bystanders in this process. As they engage in verbal thrashings of the laboratory and their fellow experimenters, they are presently contributing less to empathy and more to the public's alienation and withdrawal from politics.

Again, the signals are mixed here, but they don't point consistently in a positive direction. Unfortunately, once the cycle of distrust and unhappiness with the political process have reached a critical mass, it is in the interest of elected officials to resonate with such sentiments. Reelection is served by denouncing government and politics and pledging to clean it up. It becomes politically risky to do otherwise. Yet the Lewinsky scandal may have had its impact here as well. While it alienated more citizens from the political process (and perhaps from both parties), it did raise a large warning flag to those in the laboratory who have been using scandal as a means of stopping experiments. The most prominent casualties of the scandal were those who gained national leadership positions through the use of the scandal weapon: ex–House Speaker Newt Gingrich and ex–House Speaker Bob Livingston. Livingston inherited the speakership as Gingrich fell on his sword, only to be undone a few days later by his own personal scandal.

Scandalmongering may have reached its high tide with the impeachment of President Clinton and the resignation of a Republican Speaker who became known by denouncing scandalous behavior and who used the Lewinsky affair and the Constitution for further partisan gain. It is now likely that the scandal weapon will begin to recede in the political arsenal, and as a result policy experiments will be less clouded in the laboratory. Does this change mean, however, that we can rely on political officials to try to restore some empathy in the political culture?

Perhaps, but it is more likely to come from nontraditional quarters. One key to increasing empathy may rest with the new reformist traditions within the political process. Much of that tradition today exists not at the national but at the local level. Citizen activists are attempting to make their way into the political laboratory of school boards, city councils, boards of supervisors, and state legislatures. Although their motives are not all "pure," many of them are motivated by a strong desire to do something constructive about the problems facing their communities. They are willing to get inside the political laboratory at considerable cost to their own well-being and the well-being of their families because they want to conduct new experiments they think are vital to the future of their communities. Many believe that they cannot rely on the existing experimenters for successful solutions to their communities' problems, and more still believe as well that they must reform the very process by which the experimenters are recruited and the experiments are conducted.

The new politicians would never succeed by themselves, but fortunately they are not alone. Although empathy is diminishing in the democratic process, and large numbers of people have divorced themselves from it (through either alienation or sheer disgust), substantial numbers of citizens out there are deeply desirous of finding "something better." They constitute small armies of people willing to help reform a system they no longer feel is working the way it was meant to work.

These groups most often arise locally. They are driven by a combination of a desire to improve their future and the anger that comes from having failed to get government to do the "right thing" when they depended on their representatives to have their desires translated into public policy. Their anger is based on a previous history of struggles with local issues of great significance to them and their families. These include struggles with school boards over the education of their children; conflicts over rezoning issues that posed great threats to them and their neighbors; a variety of environmental hazards previously unchecked by state and local authorities; and gang drive-bys, car-jackings, burglaries, and murders that threaten their personal security.

These problems are nearly universal in today's modern cities. They cut across geography, region, ethnicity, and wealth. Consequently, activists and their "armies" are emerging from Latino, African American, and white parts of communities. Neighborhood associations are forming in both poor and rich sections of cities, and neighborhood watch programs are seen in every quarter.

Such movements don't occur in a vacuum. They require large numbers of citizens committed to the cause and individuals who are willing to organize and lead. No wonder, then, that in the midst of all this ferment, new leadership is emerging, challenging the present occupants in the political laboratory, demanding new experiments and a better experimental process. The "armies" are large enough to win skirmishes and even wars at the local level, and are large enough to challenge local party structures and local economic elites. These new reformists are getting elected to school boards, city councils, state legislatures, and county boards of supervisors.

They are part of the greatness of the American dream. Only in America are there substantial numbers of citizens who still believe that if they get angry enough, are willing to work hard enough, and can marshal enough of their friends and like-minded neighbors, they can make a difference in charting the future. They still believe that in America, citizens—not the political and economic elite—can take power back from those who govern.

And in some ways they have. It is because of them that recycling strategies have been implemented across the nation. It is because of their vigilance that ecological disasters inside urban areas are being minimized. It is because of them that there is a return to neighborhood-based policing strategies and successful neighborhood watch programs.

And it is through them that campaign finance reform has been implemented in scores of cities and states.

The new reformists can create empathy in two ways. First, they can do so indirectly through their reformist agenda. They seek reform not only through new and better public policies but also through changes in the structure of the political laboratory (for example, through campaign finance reform and term limits). In doing so, they place emphasis on what is going on inside the laboratory. Shining the spotlight in such a way may encourage others—including the media—to focus on the conditions under which experiments are taking place.

They can also create empathy in a second and more direct manner. These new reformists and their armies of volunteers practice "open politics." Once in office, they tend to keep in close touch with their supporters, engaging them in various aspects of the political laboratory and expanding patterns of citizen participation at the local level. Part of the army ends up serving on boards and commissions, task forces, advisory groups, and myriad other direct contacts with the laboratory itself. Typically, citizens emerge from these experiences wiser and more knowledgeable about the complexities of policy making and the use of scarce resources. Thus, and perhaps inadvertently, these new reformists are expanding significantly the numbers of people who are able to empathize with what is going on inside the political system.

To what extent can these reformists bring about reform and create greater empathy at the national, as opposed to the local, level? The road there is much tougher to navigate. On the one hand, their most popular issues will quickly be co-opted, at least rhetorically. For example, Earth Day was an annual attempt to publicize the fragile nature of our ecology and to create awareness and local response to environmental problems. In hundreds of cities, environmental activists marched on a Sunday in April and conducted workshops on everything from recycling and composting to education and lobbying strategies. Today, many members of the U.S. Congress who oppose comprehensive environmental protections lead off the annual parade, and some of the worst corporate polluters are now publicly sponsoring and helping to fund Earth Day. In an ironic twist in my community, the last Earth Day pageant was led by a local congressman who voted against most environmental protections in Congress. The parade was sponsored by a company that, for decades, was a major polluter in the community. Many of the grassroots environ-

mental groups in the community boycotted the very Earth Day cele-
brations they helped to start years ago.

Likewise, many national politicians are co-opting several essentially
local issues, over which they have little control, to curry favor with
those who have fought for them. A major spawning ground for the new
reformers has been urban sprawl and the negative consequences of
rezoning. Though he was not the only one, Al Gore, when he was vice-
president, began to articulate a rhetorical strategy of targeting such
problems at the national level even though such issues have historically
been the province of local government.

Such co-opting is not new in American politics; in fact, quite the
contrary. It recognizes the importance of new movements and their
potential significance for the political process. Co-opting is one way of
garnering votes and expanding political coalitions, but it is done for
another reason as well: to keep the new reformers out of power. The
reformers, meanwhile, are finding that there is a huge difference between succeeding at the local level and succeeding at the national level.

A number of factors make it difficult for the new reformers to move
from the local to the national level. First, since they often take on
economic as well as political elites with their reforms, securing funding
for congressional campaigns is highly problematic. While the "army" is
available for such campaigns, it is easily overcome by the enormous
amount of funds for campaign contributions available to other candidates. Reformers seldom emerge out of the local context with war
chests and ready contributors. They learn quickly that, in the absence of
national campaign finance reform, getting elected to the national political laboratory requires levels of funding that are typically unavailable for
their efforts.

Second, some of the strategies for overcoming moneyed special interests at the local level are not available at the level of the congressional
district. Reformers and their armies learn to mobilize neighborhoods
and environmental groups and to canvass large parts of their communities through volunteers. These strategies can offset expensive television and radio commercials only when there is direct contact with
voters, and this contact is reinforced by more direct contact. Much of
this type of grassroots activity can be accomplished in large part because
the playing field is relatively compact and walking strategies are feasible.
Only in very rare instances is that the case in congressional districts.

Some districts for Congress encompass an entire state (for instance, Alaska, Delaware, Montana, North Dakota, Vermont, and Wyoming). Others stretch for hundreds of miles. Direct voter contact is virtually impossible, and the value of "armies" is minimized and often destroyed by the power of television, radio, and direct mail advertising strategies.

Third, the sheer size of congressional districts means that another weapon is lost: free publicity through the media. Twenty-five or thirty different local television stations, dozens of radio news stations, and as many as ten different newspapers may make up the "media" of a congressional district. Simply coordinating a free media strategy becomes awesome and far more complicated than when the focus is on generating attention for a specific cause inside a smaller media market. And because the object of attention—Washington, D.C.—is farther away, so is the attention by news gatherers. You can attend the council meeting at city hall, pack the chambers, demand attention for your issue, and expect to get coverage. It is much harder to accomplish the same thing at the national level when you are in a congressional district that is many hundreds or thousands of miles from Washington, D.C.

Finally, local elections are low-turnout elections. Perhaps a third of potential voters will cast their ballots in a non-presidential year for a congressional race. As low as that sounds, it is not unlikely that only 20 percent or even 15 percent of potential voters will vote in a local race. The universe of local voters is easier to address: They are fewer in number, but perhaps they vote because they are far more aware of the issues than their non-voting counterparts.

For all of these reasons, many successful reformists will not get to Congress, and certainly not on the terms that allowed them to exercise power in their local communities. While they may increase the empathy of the public at the local level, it is not likely that they will have much impact on the level of empathy toward politicians who conduct experiments at the national level.

The end of my story begins here, in the reformist tradition. I became active in the political process by trying to reform both public policies and the laboratory itself, and I've spent nearly a quarter of a century doing so. During that time, I've tried to lead three lives: a professional one, a family one, and a political one. It's been virtually impossible, and I've paid for it, but fortunately I've not been alone. Through all the city council and mayoral races, I've been accompanied by an army of dedicated citizens equally committed to making the system "work right." Like me, they gave of their extraordinarily limited time until they could no longer give. They licked envelopes, they walked streets on hot days, and they supported my campaigns financially even when their own finances were in dire straits. And they kept the faith that things would change. Once I was inside the political laboratory, they gave again: serving on boards and commissions, holding rump sessions on public policy problems, and rooting me on.

Backed by an army of reformist supporters, my focus eventually turned from the local level to the national. After working in the local laboratory long enough, you come to understand that no city exists in a vacuum, and no city can be inoculated from the experiments being conducted at the national level. And so, twice I've run for the U.S. Congress, and both times I missed by the narrowest of margins. In so doing, I twice learned about the difference between the success of reformists at the local level and their ability to get inside the national political laboratory. Despite huge armies of supporters, despite the good wishes and continued allegiance of those who had been there all the previous times, despite all the hard work, and despite the broad support from the city in which I live, I still lost.

Trying to reform both the experiments and the nature of the national laboratory, I ran on a clear set of policies, limited my spending, refused to accept special-interest contributions, and worked with hundreds of volunteers to overcome the entrenched power of moneyed interests that underwrite most congressional campaigns. In my first race I ran in a congressional district that spans 300 miles and includes nearly 500,000 people. I was outspent by a nearly 4-to-1 margin. I drove around the district until my car was barely running. I lost by 1,200 votes.

In my second campaign I did 200 coffees in an attempt to balance out the power of money being pumped into the incumbent's coffers by Washington-based, narrow special interests. I raised about $300,000, overwhelmingly from small contributors, but I was outspent by a 3-to-1 margin by my opponent. I received no support from the national political party, and running in an off-year election, the incumbent enjoyed all the advantages. I lost once more, and once more the outcome was very close. Afterward, everywhere I went I was complimented on the quality of the campaign, and almost everyone I encountered told me that they had voted for me. In fact, I started to believe that the incumbent won without anyone voting for him.

My campaigns were overcome both times by an avalanche of money, much of it from special-interest political action committees. Neither the large size of my "army" nor my commitment to eighteen-hour workdays and hundreds of coffees and speeches was able to overcome what money can buy in certain types of elections. The results of all that work were only two: the consolation that I came very close, and the wonderful feedback I received about the "conduct" of the campaigns. My experience further underlined how difficult it is to change the political laboratory in Washington.

Yet I tried twice, knowing the obstacles, and as I write this, my core supporters just raised the first $50,000 to convince me to try again. I'm tempted. I don't know if it's just ego and the need to win or a stubborn and optimistic belief that there is indeed a way to get into the national laboratory and that I can make a difference at that level. I've known too many realistic/pessimistic politicians. We need more optimists now; reformists are all optimists.

Weighing against running again are a number of factors. I don't fear the work, but I fear the consequences of eighteen-hour days, seven days a week. I fear losing my family. They will never desert me, but I will cause them much pain, sorrow, and loss of quality time we will never recover. I fear falling short on my professional obligations. And I fear losing myself. I've had so little time in over two decades to write poems, take photographs, or chat leisurely with old friends. I took only one vacation in over two decades; I would like to take another.

So, undecided, I finish writing this book. I know that whichever decision I make, and regardless of how much I can still accomplish in office, it will not be enough. It will take much more to return empathy to the political culture than the actions of one person (even with a local army of reformers). Yet I wouldn't be a political animal if I didn't finish with some parting advice to my fellow citizens:

- Please try to look hard and long into the laboratory before you make judgments about what officials are and are not doing.
- Be skeptical of politicians who run for reelection and denounce the very institution in which they want to represent you. Be equally skeptical when politicians and the media use slander and accuse oth-

ers of scandal rather than keeping their eyes on the experiments in the laboratory.

- Don't accept simplistic solutions to complex problems, and don't accept simplistic explanations from the media of why things are happening inside the political laboratory.
- Demand coverage of the laboratory from the news gatherers. Encourage them to probe further into what policy makers do and how they do it.
- Get active! Get involved with neighborhood associations. Volunteer for boards and commissions. Work with your local school. If need be, petition your representatives and contact them about what you want done in the laboratory. Join a bowling league; at least talk regularly with your neighbors.
- Get involved in political campaigns. If you don't like the people running, get one of your own to run, but get involved directly in the process that decides how you will be represented.
- Do whatever you can about campaign finance reform. It can be as easy as this: Don't vote for any candidate who takes contributions from political action committees; don't vote for any candidate who spends more than $500,000 on a congressional district race. Remember—the money most likely is not being spent for good government but to further narrow self-interest.

My suggestions are not easy to follow. They are time-consuming, and they thrust people into realms of activity that produce conflict and dissonance. But I don't know if we have any choice. The new millennium we've entered will not give us easy answers about our own lives or the society around us. It is a truism that democracy itself is complicated and doesn't come cheap. We will need to redouble our efforts to create the type of empathy needed to guarantee that our form of democracy will survive in the next millennium.

NOTES

1. *The Larry King Show,* June 15, 1993.

2. Daniel J. Boorstein, *The Lost World of Thomas Jefferson* (Chicago: University of Chicago Press, 1993).

3. Robert D. Putnam, "The Prosperous Community: Social Capital and Public Life," *The American Prospect* 13 (1993): 36.

4. Suzanne L. Parker and Glenn R. Parker, "Why Do We Trust Our Congressman?" *Journal of Politics* 55 (1993): 442–453.

5. Robin Toner, "Image of Capitol Maligned by Outsiders, and Insiders," *New York Times,* October 16, 1994.

6. Tim Wirth, "Diary of a Senator," *New York Times Magazine,* August 9, 1992, pp. 16–24.

7. John J. DiIulio, Donald F. Kettl, and Richard P. Nathan, "Making Health Reform Work," *The Brookings Review* 12 (1994): 22–25.

8. The classic study is by Virginia Sapiro, "Private Costs of Public Commitments or Public Costs of Private Commitments? Family Roles versus Political Ambition," *American Journal of Political Science* 26 (1982): 265–279.

9. Ibid., p. 277.

10. James W. Clarke and Marcia M. Donovan, "Personal Needs and Political Incentives: Some Observations on Self-Esteem," *American Journal of Political Science* 24 (1980): 545, 547.

11. Ibid., pp. 542–543.

12. Gwen Ifill, "Democrats Drop Breakfast Costing $15,000 a Couple," *New York Times,* May 25, 1993.

13. Suzanne Garment, *Scandal: The Culture of Mistrust in American Politics* New York: Times Books, 1991.

14. *The Vic Caputo Show,* June 14, 1993.

15. National Public Radio, June 15, 1993.

16. Dorothy J. Samuels, "Ways and Means: Dan Rostenkowski's Feathered Life Style," *New York Times,* June 13, 1993.

17. Udayan Gupta and Brent Bowers, "When It Comes to Pay, Heads of Little Firms Can Outdo Top CEOs," *Wall Street Journal,* July 20, 1993; John W. Wright, *The American Almanac of Jobs and Salaries* (New York: Avon Books, 1992–98).

18. Jonathan D. Salant, "Big Spenders Did Well in '98 Vote," Associated Press, December 30, 1998.

19. California Commission on Campaign Financing, *Money and Politics: Financing California's Local Elections* (Los Angeles: Center for Responsive Government, 1989), p. 6.

20. Neil A. Lewis, "Lawmakers Sow Health Bills and Reap Big Donations," *New York Times,* May 23, 1994.

21. California Commission on Campaign Financing, *Money and Politics: Financing California's Local Elections* (Los Angeles: Center for Responsive Government, 1989), p. 15.

22. *Hot Talk with Charles Adler,* June 23, 1993.

23. Remark attributed by nearly everyone in Arizona to former U.S. congressman Morris K. Udall.

24. Jay Leno, quoted in "Arkansas Town of Flippin Is Celebrating the Whitewater Affair Because of the Media Interest," *New York Times,* March 19, 1993.

25. These include land-use planning, transportation, criminal justice, economic development, law enforcement, federal and state legislative and political processes, election law, recreation programs, public education, cultural and minority relations, budgeting processes, health issues, environmental problems, landfill and recycling issues, funding strategies involved with infrastructure improvements, effective methods of neighborhood preservation and enhancement, citizen participation processes, strategies for public-private partnerships, personnel policies and problems, housing strategies, and the problems of the homeless.

26. Anonymous telephone call to Mayor and Council Answering Service (a recording procedure designed to solicit comments after hours from citizens to the governing body of the city).

27. There is an excellent discussion of this problem in John E. Schwarz, *Illusions of Opportunity: The American Dream in Question* (New York: W. W. Norton, 1997).

28. "Government Malperformance," *Public Perspective* (Roper Center for Public Opinion Research), 4 (July/August 1993): 98–99.

29. Christopher Jencks, *The Homeless* (Cambridge: Harvard University Press, 1994), p. 19.

30. John I. Gilderbloom, "Trends in the Affordability of Rental Housing: 1970 to 1983," *Sociology of Social Research* 70 (1986): 301–302.

31. David A. Snow and Leon Anderson, *Down on Their Luck: A Study of Homeless Street People* (Berkeley: University of California Press, 1993).

32. Ibid., p. 255.

33. If policy makers are meeting behind closed doors (and there is nothing unusual about their meeting behind closed doors), then there is not much news unless the reporter has reliable reports of their actual activities.

BIBLIOGRAPHY

There is a great deal of literature in political science on democratic theory and practice, on political parties and elections, on civic culture and political participation, and on governance. Apart from the "kiss and tell stories" written by present and former politicians, there is far less on the lives led by those in the political laboratory. I am heavily indebted in writing this book to the literature listed below.

Aberbach, Joel D., Robert D. Putnam, and Bert A. Rockman. *Bureaucrats and Politicians in Western Democracies.* Cambridge: Harvard University Press, 1981.

Adrian, Charles R., and Michael R. Fine. *State and Local Politics.* Chicago: Lyceum Books, 1991.

Alexander, Herbert. *Reform and Reality: The Financing of State and Local Campaigns.* New York: The Twentieth Century Fund Press, 1991.

Almond, Gabriel Abraham, and Sydney Verba. *The Civic Culture: Political Attitudes and Democracy in Five Nations.* Newbury Park, N.J.: Sage Publications, 1989.

————, eds. *The Civic Culture Revisited.* Newbury Park, Calif.: Sage Publications, 1989.

"American Survey: The Solitary Bowler." *The Economist,* February 18, 1995, pp. 21–22.

Ansolabehere, Stephen, Roy Behr, and Shanto Iyengar. *The Media Game: American Politics in the Television Age.* New York: Macmillan, 1993.

Asbell, Bernard. *The Senate Nobody Knows.* Garden City: Doubleday, 1978.

Associated Press. "Debate over Health Care Enriched Campaign Coffers," May 19, 1993.

Baldassare, Mark. "Trust in Local Government." *Social Science Quarterly* 66 (1985): 704–712.

Barber, James David. *The Lawmakers: Recruitment and Adaptation of Legislative Life.* New Haven: Yale University Press, 1965.

Barone, Michael, Grant Ujifusa, and Douglas Matthews. *The Almanac of American Politics.* Boston: Gambit, 1992–1997.

Baskerville, Stephen. "Civic Education, Political Science, and Education Reform in Central Europe." *P.S.: Political Science & Politics* 30: (1997): 114–15.

Beck, Paul Allen, Hal G. Rainey, Keith Nicholls, and Carol Traut. "Citizen Views of Taxes and Services: A Tale of Three Cities." *Social Science Quarterly* 68 (1987): 223–243.

Bell, Daniel. "The Old War." *The New Republic,* August 23, 1993, pp. 18–22.

Benneth, W. Lance. *The Governing Crisis: Media, Money and Marketing in American Elections.* New York: St. Martin's Press, 1992.

Bennett, Stephen E. "Why Young Americans Hate Politics, and What We Should Do about It." *P.S.: Political Science & Politics* 30 (1997): 47–52.

Berke, Richard L. "Talk of Campaign Finance Laws Sets Off a Scramble for Donations." *New York Times,* August 13, 1993.

———. "Health Debate Is Filling Campaign Coffers." *New York Times,* April 19, 1994.

———. "U.S. Voters Focus on Selves, Poll Says." *New York Times,* September 21, 1994.

Black, Gordon S. "A Theory of Political Ambition: Career Choices and the Role of Structural Incentives." *American Political Science Review* 66 (1972): 114–159.

Bohanon, Cecil. "The Economic Correlates of Homelessness in Sixty Cities." *Social Science Quarterly* 72 (1991): 816–825.

Bok, Derek C. *The Cost of Talent: How Executives and Professionals Are Paid and How It Affects America.* New York: Free Press, 1993.

Boorstein, Daniel J. *Democracy and Its Discontents.* New York: Random House, 1974.

———. *Hidden History: Exploring Our Secret Past.* New York: Random House, 1987.

———. *The Lost World of Thomas Jefferson.* Chicago: University of Chicago Press, 1993.

Bullock, Charles S., III, and Susan A. MacManus. "Municipal Election Structure and the Election of Councilwomen." *Journal of Politics* 53 (1991): 75–89.

Burns, Bobby. *Shelter: One Man's Journey from Homelessness to Hope.* Tucson: University of Arizona Press, 1998.

Burns, Nancy. *The Formation of American Local Government: Private Values in Public Institutions.* New York: Oxford University Press, 1994.

Bycel, Benjamin. "Doing the Health-Care Hustle." *New York Times,* July 31, 1993.

California Commission on Campaign Financing. *Money and Politics: Financing California's Local Elections.* Los Angeles: Center for Responsive Government, 1989.

Canon, David T. "Sacrificial Lambs or Strategic Politicians? Political Amateurs in U.S. House Elections." *American Journal of Political Science* 37 (1993): 1119–1141.

Clark, Janet, Charles D. Hadley, and R. Darcy. "Political Ambition among Men and Women State Party Leaders: Testing the Countersocialization Perspective." *American Politics Quarterly* 14 (1989): 549–565.

Clarke, James W., and Marcia M. Donovan. "Personal Needs and Political Incentives: Some Observations on Self-Esteem." *American Journal of Political Science* 24 (1980): 536–552.

Clawson, Dan, Alan Neustadtl, and Denise Scott. *Money Talks: Corporate PACs and Political Influence.* New York: Basic Books, 1992.

Conlan, Timothy J. "Federal, State, or Local? Trends in the Public's Judgment." *The Public Perspective,* January/February 1993, pp. 3–5.

Conover, Pamela J., and Stanley Feldman. "Candidate Perceptions in an Ambiguous World: Campaigns, Cues, and Inference Processes. *American Journal of Political Science* 33 (1989): 917–940.

Cook, Timothy E. *Making Laws and Making News: Media Strategies in the U.S. House of Representatives.* Washington, D.C.: The Brookings Institution, 1989.

Costantini, Edmond. "Political Women and Political Ambition: Closing the Gender Gap." *American Journal of Political Science* 34 (1990): 741–770.

Davis, Mike. "Death and Taxes: The Sky Falls on Compton." *The Nation* 259/8 (1994): 268–271.

DeParle, Jason. "Report to Clinton Sees Vast Extent of Homelessness." *New York Times,* February 17, 1994.

DiIulio, John J., Donald F. Kettl, and Richard P. Nathan. "Making Health Reform Work." *The Brookings Review* 12 (1994): 22–25.

Dionne, E. J. *Why Americans Hate Politics.* New York: Simon and Schuster, 1991.

Drew, Elizabeth. *Senator.* New York: Simon and Schuster, 1978.

Drozdiak, William. "Revving Up Europe's Four Motors: Up and Coming City-States Are Driving the Continent's Economy." *Washington Post,* March 27, 1994.

Ehrenhalt, Alan. *The United States of Ambition.* New York: Times Books, 1991.

Eisinger, Peter K. *The Rise of the Entrepreneurial State: State and Local Economic Development Policy in the United States.* Madison: University of Wisconsin Press, 1988.

Elshtain, Jean Bethke. *Democracy on Trial.* New York: Basic Books, 1995.

Farnham, Paul G., and Stephen N. Bryant. "Form of Local Government: Structural Policies of Citizen Choice." *Social Science Quarterly* 66 (1985): 387–400.

Flanigan, William H., Wendy M. Rahn, and Nancy H. Zingale. "Political Parties as Objects of Identification and Orientation." Presented at the annual meeting of the Western Political Science Association, Salt Lake City, March 1989.

Frant, Howard. "Rules and Governance in the Public Sector: The Case of Civil Service." *American Journal of Political Science* 37 (1993): 990–1007.

Fukuyama, Francis. *The End of History and the Last Man.* New York: Avon Books, 1992.

Garment, Suzanne. *Scandal: The Culture of Mistrust in American Politics.* New York: Times Books, 1991.

Garreau, Joel. *Edge City: Life on the New Frontier.* New York: Doubleday, 1991.

Gilderbloom, John I. "Trends in the Affordability of Rental Housing: 1970 to 1983." *Sociology of Social Research* 70 (1986): 301–302.

Glaberson, William. "Trying to Unravel Health-Care Issues for Readers." *New York Times,* May 25, 1993.

———. "The Capitol Press vs. the President: Fair Coverage or Unreined Adversity?" *New York Times,* June 17, 1993.

"GOP Fund-Raising Dangerously Like Demo Access Selling They Criticize." *Arizona Daily Star* (Tucson), March 14, 1997.

"Government Malperformance." *Public Perspective* (Roper Center for Public Opinion Research) 4 (July/August 1993): 87–99.

Greeley, Andrew. "The Other Civic America: Religion and Social Capital." *The American Prospect,* 32 (1997): 68–73.

Greider, William. *Who Will Tell the People? The Betrayal of American Democracy.* New York: Simon and Schuster, 1992.

Gross, Martin L. *The Government Racket: Washington Waste from A to Z.* New York: Bantam Books, 1992.

Gupta, Udayan, and Brent Bowers. "When It Comes to Pay, Heads of Little Firms Can Outdo Top CEOs." *Wall Street Journal,* July 20, 1993.

Hibbing, John R. *Congressional Careers: Contours of Life in the U.S. House of Representatives.* Chapel Hill: University of North Carolina Press, 1991.

Ifill, Gwen. "Democrats Drop Breakfast Costing $15,000 a Couple." *New York Times,* May 25, 1993.

Inglehart, Ronald. *Culture Shift in Advanced Industrial Society.* Princeton, N.J.: Princeton University Press, 1990.

Iyengar, Shanto. *Is Anyone Responsible? How Television Frames Political Issues.* Chicago: University of Chicago Press, 1994.

Jacobson, Gary C., and Michael A. Dimock. "Checking Out: The Effects of Bank Overdrafts on the 1992 House Elections." *American Journal of Political Science* 38 (1994): 601–624.

Jacoby, William G. "The Impact of Party Identification on Issue Attitudes." *American Journal of Political Science* 32 (1988): 643–661.

Jamieson, Kathleen Hall. *Dirty Politics: Deception, Distraction, and Democracy.* New York: Oxford University Press, 1992.

Jencks, Christopher. *The Homeless.* Cambridge: Harvard University Press, 1994.

Johansen, Elaine R. *Political Corruption: Scope and Resources.* New York: Garland Publishing, 1990.

Kahan, Michael. *Media as Politics: Theory, Behavior, and Change in America.* Upper Saddle River, N.J.: Prentice Hall, 1999.

Kanniss, Phyllis. *Making Local News.* Chicago: University of Chicago Press, 1991.

Karnig, Albert K., and Oliver Walter. "Election of Women to City Councils." *Social Science Quarterly* 56 (1976): 605–613.

Karnig, Albert K., and Susan Welsh. "Sex and Ethnic Differences in Municipal Representation." *Social Science Quarterly* 60 (1979): 465–481.

Kelman, Steven. *Making Public Policy: A Hopeful View of American Government.* New York: Basic Books, 1987.

Kornberg, Allan, and Harold D. Clarke. *Citizens and Community: Political Support in a Representative Democracy.* New York: Cambridge University Press, 1992.

Kotler, Philip. *Marketing Management.* Englewood Cliffs, N.J.: Prentice Hall, 1987.

Krason, Jonathan S., and Donald Philip Green. "Stopping the Buck Here: The Case for Campaign Spending Limits." *The Brookings Review* 11 (1993): 17–21.

Krauss, Clifford. "Lawmakers' Legal Aid Society: Rich Donors." *New York Times,* August 13, 1993.

Ladd, Everett C. "Thinking about America." *The Public Perspective* 4 (July/August 1993): 19–27.

Lau, Richard L. "Two Explanations for Negativity Effects in Political Behavior." *American Journal of Political Science* 29 (1985): 119–138.

Lewis, Neil A. "Lawmakers Sow Health Bills and Reap Big Donations." *New York Times,* May 23, 1994.

Lienesch, Michael. "Wo (e)begon (e) Democracy." *American Journal of Political Science* 36 (1992): 1004–1014.

Lijphart, Arend. *Democracies: Patterns of Majoritarian and Consensus Government in Twenty-one Countries.* New Haven: Yale University Press, 1984.

Lowery, David. "After the Tax Revolt: Some Positive, If Unintended Consequences." *Social Sciences Quarterly* 67 (1986): 736–750.

Makinson, Larry. *The Price of Admission: Campaign Spending in the 1994 Elections.* Washington, D.C.: Center for Responsive Politics, 1995.

Mangleby, David B., and Candice J. Nelson. *The Money Chase: Congressional Campaign Finance Reform.* Washington, D.C.: The Brookings Institution, 1990.

March, James G. "Preferences, Power, and Democracy." In *Power, Inequality and Democratic Politics,* Ian Shapiro and Grant Reeher, eds. Boulder: Westview Press, 1988.

Mathews, Tom. "The Lessons of Bobby." *Newsweek,* May 31, 1993, pp. 26–28.

Meier, Kenneth J., and Thomas M. Holbrook. "I Seen My Opportunities and I Took 'Em: Political Corruption in the American States." *Journal of Politics* 54 (1992): 135–155.

Moore, Michael K., and John R. Hibbing. "Is Serving in Congress Fun Again? Voluntary Retirements from the House Since the 1970s." *American Journal of Political Science* 36 (1992): 824–828.

Mueller, John. "Democracy and Ralph's Pretty Good Grocery: Elections, Equality and the Minimal Human Being." *American Journal of Political Science* 36 (1992): 983–1003.

Muller, Edward N., and Mitchell A. Seligson. "Civic Culture and Democracy: The Question of Causal Relationships." *American Political Science Review* 88 (1994): 635–653.

The Municipal Year Book. Washington, D.C.: International City Managers Association, 1934–1999.

Mutz, Diana C. "Mass Media and the Depoliticization of Personal Experience." *American Journal of Political Science* 36 (1992): 483–508.

Norris, Pippa. *Critical Citizens: Global Support for Democratic Governance.* Oxford: Oxford University Press, 1999.

Nye, Joseph S., Philip D. Zelikow, and David C. King. *Why People Don't Trust Government.* Cambridge: Harvard University Press, 1997.

Owen, Diana. "Politics and 'The Last Frontier': The Talk Radio Audience and the 1992 Presidential Election." Paper prepared for presentation at the annual meeting of the Midwest Political Science Association, Chicago, April 1993.

Pachon, Harry, and Louis DeSipio. "Latino Elected Officials in the 1990's." *P.S.: Political Science & Politics* 25 (1992): 212–217.

Parker, Suzanne L., and Glenn R. Parker. "Why Do We Trust Our Congressman?" *Journal of Politics* 55 (1993): 442–453.

Patterson, Thomas E. *Out of Order.* New York: Knopf, 1993.

Payne, James L., Oliver H. Woshinsky, Eric P. Veblen, William H. Coogan, and Gene E. Bigler. *The Motivation of Politicians.* Chicago: Nelson-Hall, 1984.

Phillips, Kevin. *The Politics of Rich and Poor: Wealth and the American Electorate in the Reagan Aftermath.* New York: Random House, 1990.

Pierce, Neal R., with Curtis W. Johnson and John Stuart Hall. *Citistates: How Urban America Can Prosper in a Competitive World.* Washington, D.C.: Seven Locks Press, 1993.

"Political Solitaire: How Special Interest Campaign Contributions Have Put an End to Competitive Elections." *Public Citizen,* Parts 1 and 2. Washington, D.C.: Public Citizen's Congress Watch, 1993.

Popkin, Samuel. *The Reasoning Voter.* Chicago: University of Chicago Press, 1991.

Postman, Neil. *Amusing Ourselves to Death: Public Discourse in the Age of Show Business.* New York: Viking, 1985.

Putnam, Robert D. "The Prosperous Community: Social Capital and Public Life." *The American Prospect* 13 (1993): 35–42.

———. "Bowling Alone: America's Declining Social Capital." *Journal of Democracy,* January 1995, pp. 65–78.

Putnam, Robert D., Robert Leonardi, and Raffaella Nanetti. *Making Democracy Work: Civic Traditions in Modern Italy.* Princeton, N.J.: Princeton University Press, 1993.

Rahn, Wendy M. "The Role of Partisan Stereotypes in Information Processing about Candidates." *American Journal of Political Science* 37 (1993): 497–528.

Rausch, Jonathan. *Demosclerosis: The Silent Killer of American Government.* New York: Times Books, 1994.

Ripley, Randall B., Samuel C. Patterson, Lynn M. Maurer, and Stephen V. Quinlan. "Constituents' Evaluations of U.S. House Members." *American Politics Quarterly* 20 (1995): 442–456.

Rivlin, Alice M. *Reviving the American Dream: The Economy, the States, and the Federal Government.* Washington, D.C.: Brookings Institution Press, 1991.

Rivlin, Gary. *Fire on the Prairie: Chicago's Harold Washington and the Politics of Race.* New York: Holt, 1992.

Romer, Thomas, and James M. Snyder, Jr. "An Empirical Investigation of the Dynamics of PAC Contributions." *American Journal of Political Science* 38 (1994): 745–769.

Rosenthal, Alan. *Legislative Life: People, Process, and Performance in the States.* New York: Harper and Row, 1981.

Safire, William. "Political Spouse." *New York Times,* June 24, 1993.

Salant, Jonathan D. "Big Spenders Did Well in '98 Vote." Associated Press, December 30, 1998.

Samuels, Dorothy J. "Ways and Means: Dan Rostenkowski's Feathered Life Style." *New York Times,* June 13, 1993.

Samuelson, Robert J. "Did the Press Flunk Health Care?" *Washington Post,* April 22, 1994.

———. *The Good Life and Its Discontents: The American Dream in the Age of Entitlement, 1945–1995.* New York: Times Books, 1996.

Sapiro, Virginia. "Private Costs of Public Commitments or Public Costs of Private Commitments? Family Roles versus Political Ambition." *American Journal of Political Science* 26 (1982): 265–279.

Savitch, H. V., and John Clayton Thomas, eds. *Big City Politics in Transition.* Newbury Park, Calif. 1991.

Schlesinger, Joseph. *Ambition and Politics.* Chicago: Rand McNally, 1966.

Schmitter, Phillipe C., and Terry Lynn Karl. "What Democracy Is . . . and Is Not." *Journal of Democracy* 2 (1991): 75–88.

Schneider, Mark, and Paul Teske. "Toward a Theory of the Political Entrepreneur: Evidence from Local Government." *American Political Science Review* 86 (1992): 737–747.

Schorr, Lisbeth B. "What Works: Applying What We Already Know about Successful Social Policy." *The American Prospect* 13 (1993): 43–54.

Schudson, Michael. "Voting Rites: Why We Need a New Concept of Citizenship." *The American Prospect* 19 (1994): 59–68.

Schwarz, John E. *America's Hidden Success: A Reassessment of Twenty Years of Public Policy.* New York: W. W. Norton, 1983.

———. *Illusions of Opportunity: The American Dream in Question.* New York: W. W. Norton, 1997.

Schwarz, John E., and Thomas J. Volgy. *The Forgotten Americans: Working Hard and Living Poor in the Land of Opportunity.* New York: W. W. Norton, 1992.

———. "How Economic Development Succeeds and Fails at the Same Time." *Governing* 5 (November 1992): 10–11.

Seelye, Katharine Q. "Lobbyists Are the Loudest in the Health Care Debate." *New York Times,* August 16, 1994.

Skocpol, Theda. "Associations without Members." *The American Prospect* 45 (1999): 66–73.

Snow, David A., and Leon Anderson. *Down on Their Luck: A Study of Homeless Street People.* Berkeley: University of California Press, 1993.

Starr, Paul. "Democracy v. Dollar." *The American Prospect* 31 (1997): 6–9.

Stein, Lana, and Arnold Fleischmann. "Shaking the Money Tree: Assessing Local Campaign Contributions." Paper prepared for presentation at the annual meeting of the Midwest Political Science Association, Chicago, April 1994.

Sullivan, John L., James Piereson, and George E. Marcus. *Political Tolerance and American Democracy.* Chicago: University of Chicago Press, 1993.

Task Force on Campaign Finance Reform. *Campaign Finance Reform: Insights and Evidence.* Princeton, N.J.: Woodrow Wilson School of Public and International Affairs, 1998.

Thayer, George. *Who Shakes the Money Tree? American Campaign Financing Practices from 1789 to the Present.* New York: Simon and Schuster, 1973.

Thompson, Dennis F. "Mediated Corruption: The Case of the Keating Five." *American Political Science Review* 87 (1993): 369–382.

Toner, Robin. "Streamlining the Ungainly." *New York Times Magazine,* July 25, 1993, pp. 12, 14.

———. "Health Impasse Sours Voters, New Poll Finds." *New York Times,* September 13, 1994.

———. "Image of Capitol Maligned by Outsiders, and Insiders." *New York Times,* October 16, 1994.

Verba, Sydney, Kay Lehman Schlozman, and Henry E. Brady. *Voice and Equality: Civic Voluntarism in American Politics.* Cambridge: Harvard University Press, 1995.

———. "The Big Tilt: Participatory Inequality in America." *The American Prospect* 32 (1997): 74–80.

Wattenberg, Martin P. *The Rise of Candidate-Centered Politics: Presidential Elections of the 1980s.* Cambridge: Harvard University Press, 1991.

Welsh, Susan. "Women as Political Animals? A Test of Some Explanations for Male-Female Political Participation Differences." *American Journal of Political Science* 21 (1977): 711–730.

Welsh, Susan, and Albert K. Karnig. "Correlates of Female Office-Holding in City Politics." *Journal of Politics* 41 (1979): 478–491.

Wertheimer, Fred. "Independent Expenditures and the Response-Time Provision of S. 999, the Clean Campaign Act of 1989." Testimony given before the U.S. Senate Committee on Commerce, Science, and Transportation, July 19, 1989. Washington, D.C.: Government Printing Office, pp. 1–12.

Wiegele, Thomas C., and Kent Layne Oots. "Type A Behavior and Local Government Elites." *Political Psychology* 11 (1990): 721–737.

Williams, Shirley, and Edward L. Lascher. *Ambition and Beyond: Career Paths of American Politicians.* Berkeley: University of California Press, 1993.

Wines, Michael. "Mud on the House Floor: It's a Glimpse of Democracy in Action, but It's Not a Pretty Sight." *New York Times,* May 28, 1993.

Wirth, Tim. "Diary of a Senator." *New York Times Magazine,* August 9, 1992, pp. 16–24.

Wright, John W. *The American Almanac of Jobs and Salaries.* New York: Avon Books, 1992–1998.

ABOUT THE AUTHOR

Thomas J. Volgy was born in Hungary and escaped with his family to America at the age of nine. He received his Ph.D. in political science from the University of Minnesota. He is a professor in the political science department of the University of Arizona, where he has been honored for both his teaching and his public service. He has published dozens of articles in professional journals of the discipline and in national magazines, including *The New Republic, The American Prospect,* and *The Nation.* His previous book, *The Forgotten Americans,* co-authored with John E. Schwarz, received national awards and recognition after its publication.

In addition to his professional obligations, Volgy served for fourteen years in elected office on the Tucson City Council and as mayor of Tucson. During that time he accepted as well a national leadership role with the U.S. Conference of Mayors and the National League of Cities. He has served as a delegate to two national Democratic conventions, including membership on the Democratic National Convention's Rules Committee, and he won his party's nomination for election to Congress in 1998.

Since leaving public office, Volgy has been actively involved with the training of government officials and counter-elites overseas (including countries of the former Soviet Union, Eastern Europe, and Central America) in the areas of democratic political development and public policy. In addition, he was part of the international team that monitored Hungary's first democratic elections in the post—cold war environment. Presently he is working on a research project about the changes brought on by the end of the cold war.